Notes & Apologies:

✭ Subscriptions to *The Believer* include four issues, one of which might be themed and may come with a bonus item, such as a giant poster or art object. View our subscription deals at *thebeliever.net/subscribe.*

✭ The "Complete Me" in this issue, where readers can test their knowledge of writer Joy Williams, abandons the game's typical formatting. When we wrote Williams about possibly penning a list of trivia about her own life, she responded with the typewritten note published on page 111. Typos and letter-key malfunctions have been preserved for their obvious charm and beauty.

✭ Dispersed throughout the issue is a microinterview with writer Noor Naga, conducted by editorial assistant Ginger Greene. Naga's debut novel, *If an Egyptian Cannot Speak English*, came out in 2022 with Graywolf Press. She is also the author of *Washes, Prays*, a novel-in-verse. Naga spoke to Greene over Zoom on a Tuesday. She answered each question with enthusiastic gesticulations, holding a pen and flashing her blue-painted nails.

✭ The incidental illustrations, of agile manga superheroes, are by Masanori Ushiki.

✭ Several people have asked when we will again throw a party at the Latin American Club in San Francisco. Pronouncements on this matter will be forthcoming.

T0025913

DEAR THE BELIEVER

849 VALENCIA STREET, SAN FRANCISCO, CA 94110

letters@thebeliever.net

Dear Believer,

I have only read the first two issues since you returned but I can't help but notice each cover has featured a star from season two of *The White Lotus*. Will *The Believer* ultimately interview every actor in the show? I think I speak for all subscribers when I say I hope Jennifer Coolidge is next.

> *Sam Ransome*
> *London, UK*

Dear Believer,

I very much enjoyed John Wray's guest column on Penelope Spheeris's metal documentary (Resurrector, Summer 2023). I went out and watched the movie and also did some googling into Chris Holmes—how could I not?—to see what he was up to these days. To my relief, he's alive and sober, and it turns out he actually filmed a new version of the scene for Duke TV in 2017. I was also glad to read that he's recently been touring around Europe too. I thought other readers of Wray's column might be interested to know this. Here's to new beginnings,

> *Janie*
> *Syracuse, NY*

Dear Believer,

I'll admit that some of the finer points in Ted McDermott's story ("Adaptive Fictions," Summer 2023) went over my head. But I was glad to see you guys publishing a story at the intersection of science and philosophy. I was particularly interested in Hoffman's argument that truth and fitness are opposed—that our perceptions show us what we need to see to survive, not what is real. This intuitively made a lot of sense to me. It's a disorienting idea but, oddly, I see how it was comforting to Mr. McDermott.

I also thought it was very clever how Mr. McDermott tied these theories back into his own work with fiction, and his own use of adaptive lies. I think all great fiction has some sort of mystery at its core—some kind of koan-like quality—and that is where this story on Hoffman sort of leaves you: wrestling with the vast paradox of the whole thing. The truth is wide and deep and probably beyond the limits of our perceptions. Is this making any sense? Whenever I've talked to someone about this story, it sounds like I just took a bong rip, but I really haven't. I'm just sitting here with my cup of black tea. Anyway, thanks for publishing this piece. It stretched the neurons in good ways.

> *Will Roberts*
> *Sacramento, CA*

Dear Believer,

I really loved Joshua Hunt's article about grieving his late uncle's death ("Mount Fear Diary," Summer 2023). I recently read Studs Terkel's *Will the Circle Be Unbroken?* and one of the things that I took away from it is that a lot of people want grieving to happen fast. But we don't get to set the terms. We can't predict how long or short it will be. The only thing that is true about it is that we have to move through it—it must be done. I thought it was very wise of Mr. Hunt to concretize the experience, to give it shape. To allow it to be something real and physical and lived.

I think in the United States, very often, we don't want to look at death. We put our elders in nursing homes. We push our cemeteries to the peripheries of our cities. We don't have time for anything but the glowing efficiency of youth. Most of us have no idea how to talk about death. I count myself among these people, by the way. Death has always made me incredibly uncomfortable. So I commend Mr. Hunt for trying to work through all of this. May his uncle's memory always be a blessing. Thank you for such a beautiful piece of writing,

> *Gary L.*
> *Topeka, KS*

Dear Believer,

I liked Jim Jarmusch's (Interview, Summer 2023) comment about looking to teenagers for his inspiration. I have two teenagers and find that their concerns and perspectives are so often ignored. Meanwhile we have these ancient senators hoarding power for far too long. The kids are all right and we should definitely be listening to them more. Kudos to Mr. Jarmusch for keeping an open mind.

> *Ariel Lisker*
> *Berkeley, CA*

BLVR: So then who is a choreographer?

ABP: My most basic definition of *choreography* is the aesthetic organization of the body in space. Because if you say it's the organization of the body in space, that could be somebody who, like an engineer, would figure out where people should stand in a production line. That is *a* choreography, but I wouldn't call that person a choreographer, because there's no aesthetic.

> ## "FILM IS LIKE MUSIC: IT CREATES ITS OWN TIME." *p. 101*

BLVR: You mentioned technology. Can you tell me about your tools? Are there parts of the process that you still like to do by hand?

GLY: The most recent graphic novel that I wrote and drew, *Dragon Hoops*, was the very first time that I drew completely digitally, and I did it mostly on a Wacom tablet. I didn't use any paper at all.

> ## "EDUCATION AS A PUBLIC GOOD REMAINS AN ELUSIVE FANTASY, YET IS IT NOT AN IDEAL WORTH FIGHTING FOR?" *p. 60*

Compiled by Gabe Boyd; portraits and Charlie Chan illustrations by Kristian Hammerstad; beach chair by Madison Ketcham

BLVR: I thought a spider had been named after you. I looked it up. It's not a spider. [Consults notes] It's a tarantula-killing parasitic worm.

JD: Yes. [Smiles]

"BUT WHAT IF HOLLYWOOD STUDIOS HAD CAST AN ASIAN ACTOR IN THE ROLE OF CHARLIE CHAN INSTEAD?" *p. 81*

School bus illustration by Madison Ketcham

UNDERWAY

WE ASK WRITERS AND ARTISTS: WHAT'S ON YOUR DESK? WHAT ARE YOU WORKING ON?

by Chloé Cooper Jones

Postcard

This a postcard of a painting called The Rose by Jay DeFeo. I saw it with my mother for the first time in 2013. We were walking past the Whitney and went in on a whim and there it was. I've thought about it each day since, and it's a huge part of the book on devotion I'm writing now.

Notecards

I always keep a stack of notecards on my desk, as I often encounter an idea when reading or in conversation that is so relevant to my work that I want to concretize it in big block letters and pin it to my office wall or tape it on my computer screen. This phrase, "textual inexhaustibility," is from S/Z by Roland Barthes, and is a reminder for me to aim for work of such detail and richness that it yields a multiplicity of interpretation, resonance, and entry points— which in turn invites the reader to be a producer of and not merely a consumer of a text's meaning.

Hobonichi Diary

This is a five-year diary. I started writing in it, semi-auspiciously, in January 2020. Each page has five spaces to write about a single date over the course of five years. Revisiting where I was each day over the past few years is often an awe-inspiring exercise in just how much can change in a year and how much can stay the same.

Faith

My boyfriend, the artist and choreographer Matty Davis, recently made a work that included his exploration of the Three Sisters mountain range. While he was there, he took photographs on 35 mm film of North Sister, also referred to as "Faith," as it was being swallowed up by a storm cloud. He made this darkroom print and gifted it to me for my birthday, along with a letter that contained some questions about faith as it relates to devotion, which is the subject of my next book. This is one of my most cherished possessions, as it represents a sort of bridging of concepts that drive his artistic practice and mine.

Hammer and Nail

This broken hammer and nail are also gifts from Matty and are from a body of his work titled Amidst Endless Repetition Lies Equally Endless Variability. In this work, he used hammers and the blunt force of the body to transform thousands of standard building nails. I keep this broken hammer and nail near me as I write to remind myself that it is a familiar set of forces—death, love, grief, loss, power, searching, joy, fear, et cetera—that creates the impulse to write literature, and yet from that set of forces can come endless variability. Am I the first to write under the weight of questions of devotion? Absolutely not. Can I still make something wholly singular and unique from that blunt force? I'm trying!

I'm currently in the drafting phase of my second book and the research phase of my third, both works of nonfiction. My first book, *Easy Beauty*, attempts to take the experience of beauty—in art, nature, and other instances of aesthetic pleasure—and examine it, turning it over and over like a smooth stone in hand. My second book takes my uneasy relationship to devotion as its core concept, but is also about my decade-long obsession with a giant painting. My third book seeks to understand the feeling of kinship. The deeper I went into the writing and the thinking about these next two manuscripts, the more I realized that *Easy Beauty* was really the beginning of a longer dialogue within myself about a question of utmost importance to me. This question is, put simply: Why do we *need* art? These three books will ultimately form what I'm calling a "triptych," whose united aim will be to elucidate an argument about the relationship between making art and being human. ✶

Illustration by Kristian Hammerstad

RESURRECTOR

A ROTATING GUEST COLUMN IN WHICH WRITERS REEXAMINE CRITICALLY
UNACCLAIMED WORKS OF ART. IN THIS ISSUE: *LIZ PHAIR*

by Maris Kreizman

"I am just your ordinary, average, everyday, sane, psycho super-goddess," sings indie rock legend Liz Phair in the first song on her 2003 self-titled major-label debut. It's as if she's introducing herself to a wider audience in "Extraordinary," the cheeky opener in which she seems to be saying, *Don't worry. I may be working with hotshot producers* (the Matrix, who had recently helped launch Avril Lavigne's career) *on songs you can hear on the radio, but I'm still no normie.*

We did not go for it—neither I, the die-hard fan, nor the music critics.

Imagine me in my early twenties in New York City, trying to figure out who I was. It was the early aughts, back when jobs in the creative industries were abundant, you could still smoke in bars, and trend pieces about mainstream-rejecting, Urban Outfitters–wearing hipsters were everywhere. The least cool thing you could possibly do was aspire to be a hipster, but I didn't know that yet. Just like I didn't know that hipsterism would lead more to gentrification and commodification than to enlightenment.

Here's one thing I knew for sure, though: my love for Liz Phair was a crucial part of my identity—her 1993 album, *Exile in Guyville*, in particular. In a low, nearly monotonic voice, she sings delightfully bitter and unpretty songs accompanied by sparse instrumental backing. She sings explicitly and unabashedly about sex and romantic despair in a way that felt raw and truly subversive compared with the songs of the rest of the Lilith Fair set.

So when Phair unveiled an album of more traditionally structured songs written in a more traditional vocal range with more traditional musical backing, how could I not feel betrayed? In the present moment, when art and writing have been progressively devalued in an increasingly corporate creative world, it's funny to think back on that quaint time when selling out was the worst thing an artist could do. Fans and critics alike felt entitled to heap scorn on a musician for simply trying to broaden their appeal, or even, god forbid, to make a little more money from their art, which already wasn't especially lucrative for indie musicians, even back then.

And, oh, how I cared about what the critics had to say. My Google Reader was filled with new posts from MP3 blogs and long-established music mags alike, and it seemed like every day a new outlet cropped up. If the critics hated an album, then I hated it, too, because I believed, the critic was always right. I didn't know then that all criticism, even the most eloquently argued, is inherently subjective. The internet was allowing all sorts of new voices to take part in long-closed-off conversations, which was invigorating. But the world of music criticism, online or analog, was still very much white and male. For me to have trusted their authority above all others seems foolish now.

Back in 2003, I dismissed the new album out of hand, because what would happen to my burgeoning credibility if it turned out I… liked Liz Phair's new persona? If I allowed myself to be lured in by any catchy hook that came my way, I would show the world how unserious I was. How… *girly*.

What a relief it is, twenty years later, to trust my own ears and not give a flying fuck what anyone else thinks. Is *Liz Phair* as life-changing as *Exile in Guyville*? No. But does it contain a bunch of bangers? Oh yes. "Why Can't I?" still goes at karaoke, especially when you get to the more sexually explicit words they couldn't play on the radio. "Favorite" could be a Michelle Branch single (this is a compliment), but it's got a keen sense of humor: she compares her lover to a comfy old pair of underwear. Overall, *Liz Phair* is smart and fun and more than a little self-aware, which is way more than I could say for myself when the album first debuted. ✦

Illustration by Pete Gamlen

STUFF I'VE BEEN READING

A QUARTERLY COLUMN, STEADY AS EVER

by Nick Hornby

BOOKS READ:

* ★ *Dilla Time: The Life and Afterlife of J Dilla, the Hip-Hop Producer Who Reinvented Rhythm*—Dan Charnas
* ★ *Music Is History*—Questlove
* ★ *Ideas of Heaven: A Ring of Stories*—Joan Silber
* ★ *The Kite Runner*—Khaled Hosseini

BOOKS BOUGHT:

* ★ *Deliver Me from Nowhere: The Making of Bruce Springsteen's Nebraska*—Warren Zanes
* ★ *Shakespeare in a Divided America: What His Plays Tell Us About Our Past and Future*—James Shapiro
* ★ *Small Mercies*—Dennis Lehane
* ★ *Pied Piper*—Nevil Shute

I have occasionally vowed not to pick up any more books about music or musicians, on the grounds that I already know too much about both. For example, I know a lot more about Sam Phillips, the founder of Sun Records and the man who discovered Elvis, than I do about Proust (novels read: zero); I have read Peter Guralnick's eight-hundred-page biography of Phillips, and his magisterial two-volume Elvis biography. And I know a lot more about the Australian indie-rock band the Go-Betweens than I do about Matisse, or the reign of George IV, or most things, really. On my shelves there are *two* books that deal with the relationship between Robert Forster and Lindy Morrison of the Go-Betweens. To be fair, I own a book about Matisse, too, but I haven't actually picked it up in the eighteen years since it came out. The Forster-Morrison books were devoured almost immediately after purchase, and purchased almost immediately upon publication.

Then again, isn't this what I do and who I am? I read mostly fiction, memoirs, essays, social histories, and books about the arts, and the arts I am most drawn to are literature, film, and music. In the years remaining for me on the planet, how much of an expert on the kings and queens of Britain am I going to become? But maybe expertise isn't the point. Maybe a smattering of knowledge about everything is the way to go. But to what purpose? So that I can become a better-rounded person? I think I am doomed to being misshapen, and I should make my peace with that.

In any case, the two music books I have read recently have led me to conclude that I don't know nearly as much about music as I'd thought. Questlove's terrific new book about music and history, called—just in case you were doubting my three-word summary—*Music Is History*, is stimulating, engaged, wise. But in passing it introduced me to probably one hundred songs I didn't know before, and I now have a playlist that finds room for both Herb Alpert and Living Colour. Right now, this second, I am listening to Faze-O, a mid-'70s funk band from Dayton, Ohio; if any *Believer* reader owns a Faze-O record, they can have a free subscription to the magazine for life, on me, but you have to have kept the receipt. Dan Charnas's *Dilla Time* provided more than one playlist, and taught me more about the creation of music over the last forty years than I have ever learned from a single volume. Questlove and Charnas have both convinced me it would be stupid to switch my attention elsewhere. In the end, what we want from any book is a

Illustration by Kristian Hammerstad

new way of thinking about the world, through any prism the writer has at their disposal. And if this comes through a contemplation of music, which I love, rather than, say, a study of the brussels sprout, which, like every right-thinking person, I loathe, then why not stick to your home territory? My aim is to learn, to think differently, to become smarter, and those outcomes are just as likely through further contemplation of music—more likely, even, given that I am likely to read books about music with rapt attention.

J Dilla—Jay Dee, James Dewitt Yancey, born and raised in Detroit—made beats from samples, but his beats were unlike anyone else's beats. They were so different that Dan Charnas (whose name, incidentally, does not appear on the front cover of his book) advances the idea that "Dilla time" is a new way to describe rhythm, alongside "straight time" and "swing time." In Dilla time, component parts of the rhythm—the snare, the cymbals, the hi-hat—are manipulated so they don't land quite where they are supposed to. "It was almost as if the hi-hat was saying, 'We're going to go fifty-five miles per hour' and the snare came through right after and said, 'No, seventy miles per hour…' The effect was disorienting in a way that listening to something simply straight or solely swung wasn't. It was *elastic*—like the feeling of going faster, then slower, then faster, then slower, but never actually varying one's speed."

Why bother? Well, why bother with bebop, or cubism? Before cubism, there were all sorts of ways of depicting the world with paint. Why did we need a new one? I am hoping you regard these questions as rhetorical, by the way. That's what they are meant to be. If you're looking for answers, you have come to the wrong place. (Critical writing, it occurs to me, is full of rhetorical questions posed by critics who are terrified of being asked to provide answers.) And unlike so many artistic innovations, Dilla time hasn't led us up a blind alley. Everything started to sound like Dilla. Other producers ripped him off. Other musicians set themselves the task of learning to *play* Dilla time. Questlove—a drummer, we must remind ourselves, as well as an Oscar-winning filmmaker and writer—"had to counteract a lifetime of physical reflexes, to retrain his body to do things and feel time differently." The results can be heard best, perhaps, on D'Angelo's still-startling *Voodoo*, recorded at the turn of the century, with its loping, peg-legged, treacle-thick feel. I want to say it sounds timeless, but timing is all, and in any case, for all I know, it might sound like a Glenn Miller record to young people.

Charnas's ambition in *Dilla Time* is admirable. There is the potted history of rhythm, complete with clap-along grids and charts. There is an equally concise and comprehensible history of the drum machine. There is a narrative that runs parallel to Yancey's story, about the glories and perils of collaboration: the Soulquarians were the loose group of musicians responsible for *Voodoo*, Erykah Badu's *Mama's Gun*, and Common's *Like Water for Chocolate*; the Ummah was a production collective consisting of Dilla, A Tribe Called Quest, and others, a team that left its lopsided fingerprints on songs by Janet and Michael Jackson, the Brand New Heavies, and scores of other tracks. Who did what and who owned what caused tension and mistrust. And then there's the story of James Yancey himself, a genius, whose messy habits and personal life broke hearts, and who died, at the age of thirty-two, of a rare blood disease. I couldn't have been more stimulated by *Dilla Time*. I don't know a huge amount about hip-hop,

---

MICROINTERVIEW WITH NOOR NAGA, PART I

THE BELIEVER: You've described your experience of writing as feeling like you're one step behind your characters and following their voices through the project. Do you ever find your characters resisting the concepts and ideas you had intended to explore?

NOOR NAGA: I think resisting implies that I have an idea of where I'm going. Most of the time, I don't. So, no. Usually, I'm one step behind, letting them lead the way and then shocked by where things go. And I just have to follow along and then deal with the consequences later. But I find questions about intent to be very confusing, when people are asking, *Why did you make this choice?* I don't really think most writers make choices. ✶

but it's just music, right? (Another risky rhetorical question.) And the music was made by someone teeming with ideas, and with a breathtaking, painstaking commitment to his art, and this is as good a book about creativity as you will come across.

Questlove's book consists of chapters about every year in history from 1971 until 2001, with a chapter at the end covering the twenty-first century. The year 1976, for example, takes as its starting point "Sir Duke," Stevie Wonder's euphoric song about Duke Ellington, a single released from *Songs in the Key of Life*, his seventh album of the decade. From there it's an easy jump to some musings about Sir Duke himself and his complicated Republicanism; and to Nixon, a great Ellington admirer; and to the Bicentennial. You don't want to read about that? Why not? I don't want to know, in case you were thinking of telling me. That would mean you're not the person I thought you were. Music is the prism, but Questlove finds room for an awfully big chunk of the world. The year 1975 is Al Jarreau and the Weather Underground. The year 1983 is Reagan, the threat of nuclear warfare, the history of songs about the threat of nuclear warfare—songs by Prince, Mingus, Sun Ra—and the forgotten story of ten-year-old Samantha Smith from Maine, who wrote a letter about her fears to Soviet leader Yuri Andropov, had her letter printed in the Soviet newspaper *Pravda*, went to Moscow with her family for two weeks, appeared on the Johnny Carson show, and died in a plane crash shortly afterward. The year 1998 is the Outkast song "Rosa Parks" and the civil rights icon's rather

disappointing attempts to sue the band, which she was allowed to do despite First Amendment restrictions on the grounds that the song wasn't about her at all. All human life is here, and an awfully big chunk of Black American history. I'm not going to get any of that in "From Brussels with Love! What an Unpleasant Green Vegetable Teaches Us About Ourselves." (There is no such book… yet. If you want to write it, help yourself.)

There is very little about music in Joan Silber's *Ideas of Heaven*, first published in 2004 but only just seeing the light of day in the UK, hopefully because more and more people in my home country are discovering the writer's unique brilliance. The Italian poet Gaspara Stampa, the central and titular character in the third story here, plays the lute and sings, and there is a young gay man who sings Stampa's poems in the second story, "The High Road." But mostly these stories are about unhappy people and their angular connections to God and faith.

What Silber does do, however, if I can force the musical theme—and what else is this column, apart from themes forced upon unsuspecting and dissimilar books?—is write mixtapes. She takes a big theme—religion here; commitment to an idea in *Fools*—and writes short stories that kind of bleed into one another. That's what we used to do with cassette tapes in the days before Spotify: recording in real time allowed

---

LITERARY CLASSICS THAT HAVE NOT YET BEEN TRANSFORMED INTO MAJOR MOTION PICTURES OR TV SERIES, PART I

★ *The Catcher in the Rye* by J. D. Salinger
★ *The Golden Notebook* by Doris Lessing
★ *Invisible Man* by Ralph Ellison
★ *Blood Meridian* by Cormac McCarthy
★ *Parable of the Sower* by Octavia E. Butler
★ *Underworld* by Don DeLillo
★ *The Country of the Pointed Firs* by Sarah Orne Jewett
★ *A Confederacy of Dunces* by John Kennedy Toole
★ *A Moveable Feast* by Ernest Hemingway
★ *Song of Solomon* by Toni Morrison
★ *Pale Fire* by Vladimir Nabokov
★ *The Left Hand of Darkness* by Ursula K. Le Guin
★ *The Adventures of Augie March* by Saul Bellow
★ *The Blind Assassin* by Margaret Atwood
★ *The Crying of Lot 49* by Thomas Pynchon
★ *Death Comes for the Archbishop* by Willa Cather

—*list compiled by Gabe Boyd and Ginger Greene*

us to form ideas for the next song. I don't really miss those days, because I can now make a playlist in a few minutes, as opposed to a compilation tape in a couple of hours. But I do know my playlists aren't as good, or at least as thoughtful, as the old mixes were. Silber's stories are always surprising in the jumps they make. We are whisked from the twentieth to the fifteenth century, from China to France. I wonder whether Silber does listen to her own stories, allowing one to lead to the next, as if she were making a tape, or whether, when she has finished, she shuffles the order, like a band making an album.

The stories are always piercing and surprising. In fact, two of them end, unexpectedly, with the onrushing deaths of first-person narrators, which I'm pretty sure wouldn't be allowed in a writing class. And they are both large-hearted and extraordinarily detailed, and the themes pull you through as if you were reading a more conventional narrative. I know we're not really supposed to talk about how easy a book is to finish, but actually it's important to all of us, and I whipped through *Ideas of Heaven* as if it were a beach-read thriller.

The other fiction I read recently was Khaled Hosseini's *The Kite Runner*, first published in 2003, and not a novel in need of championing, seeing as several million people have bought it. But it is a novel that needs defending, and at the request of the book's publishers, I am helping them defend it, in a small way. Over the last twenty years it has frequently featured on a list of the books most banned by school districts and libraries in the United States, mostly because it contains a description of homosexual rape. There are also fears, according to Carnegie Mellon University's Banned Books Project, that it might inspire terrorism and "promote Islam." The rape scene is not gratuitous, needless to say. It haunts the characters in the novel for years, and it is the event on which the entire narrative turns. It's so crucial to the novel that it's hard to think of anything else that would have served the same purpose—in fact, it's hard to imagine how the novel could even exist without it. But it goes on being challenged, by parents and by school boards. Who are these parents that get upset about the books their kids are reading? If I had spotted one of my sons with his head buried in, say, *The Joy of Bestiality* or *How to Smoke Crack*, I would have been too amazed and delighted by their engagement with the written word to intervene. Needless to say, *The Kite Runner* is a book that every teenager should read. If nothing else, they would learn, paradoxically, the utter misery of living in a country where freedoms have been eroded by religious persecution. "I had thought America was against totalitarianisms," said Margaret Atwood on hearing that one of her books had been banned in Texas. "If so, surely it is important for young people to be able to recognize the signs of them. One of those signs is book-banning. Need I say more?"

There is music in *The Kite Runner*. But when the narrator returns to his home city of Kabul, now in the grips of the Taliban, it's all gone. Listen to it and read about it as much as you can, before Florida and Texas decide it's too much fun. ✳

LITERARY CLASSICS THAT HAVE NOT YET BEEN TRANSFORMED INTO MAJOR MOTION PICTURES OR TV SERIES, PART II

✳ *Falconer* by John Cheever
✳ *Pembroke* by Mary E. Wilkins Freeman
✳ *Herzog* by Saul Bellow
✳ *A House for Mr. Biswas* by V. S. Naipaul
✳ *The House on Mango Street* by Sandra Cisneros
✳ *Good Morning, Midnight* by Jean Rhys
✳ *Light in August* by William Faulkner
✳ *The Custom of the Country* by Edith Wharton
✳ *The Moviegoer* by Walker Percy
✳ *The Man Who Loved Children* by Christina Stead
✳ *Neuromancer* by William Gibson
✳ *The Years* by Virginia Woolf
✳ *Under the Net* by Iris Murdoch

—*list compiled by Gabe Boyd and Ginger Greene*

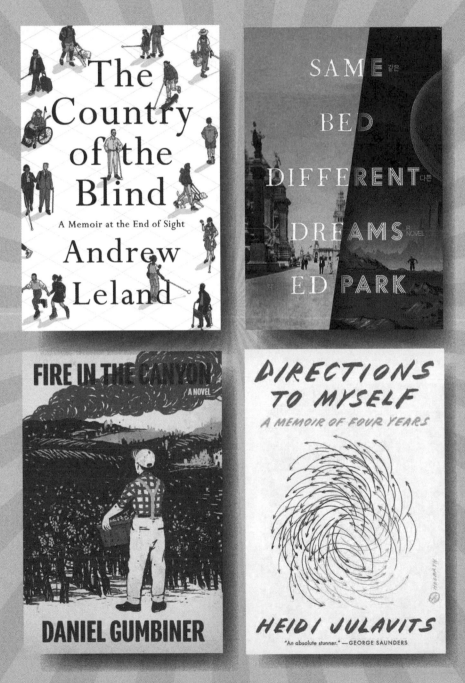

CLOSE READ

UNPACKING ONE REDOUBTABLE PASSAGE. IN THIS ISSUE:
HOW TO READ ISLAMIC CARPETS BY WALTER B. DENNY

by Mallika Rao

"**A**n outstanding example[1] of the use of the repeating[2] gül[3] can be seen in the masterwork[4] of an unknown[5] Salor Turkmen weaver, who created[6] her[7] carpet[8] in a nomadic encampment, probably in southeastern Turkmenistan,[9] in the late eighteenth century (fig. 22). The name of her tribe, Salor[10] (sometimes spelled *Salur* or *Salghur*), appears in chronicles dating back a thousand years. According to Turkmen legend, Salor women taught[11] other Turkmen tribeswomen[12] how to weave,[13] spawning one of the greatest[14] of all nomadic carpet-weaving traditions.[15]"

TURKMEN CARPET
In front of a yurt

1. Walter B. Denny, once a senior scholar in residence in the Department of Islamic Art at the Metropolitan Museum of Art, writes here of a "main carpet" in the museum's famed holdings, the largest and most valuable of Turkmen rugs, from the region of Turkmenistan. He explains by, ahem, "reading" the carpet that it was likely used on the floor of a tent of a wealthy tribal family. In part, its pinkish-magenta silk gives that provenance away— silk was an expensive fiber that had to be purchased in the marketplace, and helps impart what Denny describes as an "almost shimmering quality" to the weave.

2. The repetition of small motifs allows a weaver to proceed somewhat mechanistically: she need only memorize a pattern and keep deploying it. This weaver arranged her güls in horizontal rows and vertical columns, a.k.a., in a "stacked arrangement," staggered with "minor," or smaller, güls, which look a bit like diamonds.

3. The gül, literally "rose," a symbol of Turkmen tribes, appears as an eight-lobed medallion cut into white and red quarters and embellished with shamrocks, often with a stylized depiction of an animal at its core. Art historians date the form back more than a thousand years, speculating that it arose from an image of a lotus introduced by the Turkic people of Central Asia who practiced Buddhism before the advent of Islam. Today, this hybrid icon is woven into national identity. The flag of Turkmenistan incorporates "the gül medallions of five major tribes, the only modern national flag based on carpet forms."

4. As opposed to a painting, which can be scraped and redone to erase a painter's missteps, a carpet tells a less mediated story—of quick decisions, lagging energy, intricate game plans. Or so insists Denny, champion of the rug! "Compromises, mistakes, abandoned ideas, changes in the width of borders or the colors of motifs, and improvisations to avoid knotting one's self into

LOOM
Carpet-weaving tool

a corner—they are all there for us to see. In this sense, reading the design of a carpet is almost like taking a seat on the bench next to the weaver. It gives village and nomadic carpets a sense of human scale, human creativity, and, yes, even human frailty."

5. Denny is always enacting carpet literacy. For instance, one red rug elsewhere in the MET's collection he reads as a commercial product likely woven by boys and men in an urban workshop, while a green rug tells of a woman in a small village weaving rugs for local use or sale, incorporating designs that were hundreds of years old and passed down through generations. And then there's our rug, flush with güls and other clues suggesting it was woven by a nomadic woman of the Salor tribe, though we can't know her name.

6. Denny's read points out areas where the weaver improvised: where she was forced to modify a repetition as she reached the warp's end; where she made the güls fatter by adjusting her knots and/or inserted wefts; how the loom might have been set up; and where she might have broken some warps in the course of weaving. Sure, we know nothing about her hopes, her moods, whether a child bothered her as she worked. But the rug might inspire us to wonder.

7. While sheep shearing was undertaken by men because of the strength needed to hold a squirming animal between the knees while shaving its pelt, weaving was women's work, a way to contribute to subsistence-level nomadic economies where every effort counted. This meant folding carpet-making into domestic duties. A drop spindle could be used anywhere, at any time, and spindles have attained symbolic significance worldwide: Denny references the English term *distaff*, a type of spindle that now also connotes a woman's work, or the female side of a family.

8. So what is a carpet, anyway? Allow Denny to explain: It's a "heavy textile, made for a wide variety of utilitarian and symbolic purposes." As well, it's that rare textile meant to be used in the form in which it left the loom: never cut, pieced, joined, or tailored. Much like a sari! But good luck trying to wear a carpet.

9. The Rug Belt stretches from Morocco across North Africa, through the Middle East, and into Central Asia and northern India, and is so called because rug making flourished there as an artistic practice thanks to the region's temperate climate and land that was unfit for agriculture but perfect for sheep, whose fleece forms the rugs' fiber.

Weaving grew from a minor craft into a statewide industry from the 1600s onward, under the auspices of such empires as the Mughal and the Ottoman.

10. An ancient, possibly militaristic Turkic tribe who played an important role in Central Asian history, and whose rugs became famous in the eighteenth and nineteenth centuries.

11. How did weavers pass designs from generation to generation? With a sensible, forgiving, three-pronged creative approach, built off models, memory, and improvisation. A young weaver might have studied an older carpet while weaving a new one. More experienced weavers might have dispensed with a model altogether, if they were able to call on their memories. And everyone, no matter their age, improvised.

12. The carpet tells a broad story of female ingenuity and artistry, but it transmits small accounts too, of families, of moments shared between the women inside one. Weaving techniques and ways of finishing the ends and edges of carpets vary across geographical areas and traditions and are highly specific, passed down from mother to daughter, and from sister to sister. In theory, one can trace a specific weaving tradition to a single tent.

13. Carpets bear their own "artistic language," as Denny won't let us forget. Yes, there are the accidental stories woven into the fatness of güls, but the fluent among us can also discern trends in the religious practices of the time, as well as how taste, status, and identity operated among tribes.

14. The rug in question is "deceptively simple," Denny insists, with more colors and a more complex design than its appearance suggests, not to mention how its weave silently conveys a story of a woman coming up against the limits of her medium. That's where the word *greatest* comes in: Salor rugs—brilliantly crimson and painstakingly intricate, made with natural materials and dyes by nomadic people living in tents—are improbable creations.

15. Today many of us are blinded by the sixteenth-century Italian concept of "fine arts," which confers a higher status on drawing, painting, sculpture, and architecture. But for most of human history, certain craftspeople enjoyed the elevated status of artists, Denny tells us. Within the Islamic artistic tradition, only architecture matches the "social importance of the knotted-pile carpet." And no other Islamic art form became as well known throughout the world as the woven rug. The carpet, you could say (if you're cheesy), flies. ✭

WALTER B. DENNY

Reader of Islamic carpets

A TURKMEN "MAIN CARPET"

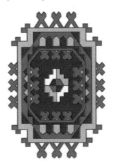

GÜL

A symbol of Turkmen tribes

ASK CARRIE

A QUARTERLY COLUMN FROM
CARRIE BROWNSTEIN, WHO IS BETTER
AT DISPENSING ADVICE THAN TAKING IT

Send questions to advice@thebeliever.net

Q: *A friend of mine is in a long-distance relationship with this guy whom she's had a crush on forever. I want her to be happy, but the relationship is toxic and she deserves better. I'm one of the few friends she vents to about it. Also, she knows I'm not completely supportive, and it's slowly driving a wedge between us. I'm afraid to be completely honest with her and possibly lose her as a friend. How do I navigate the thin line of being supportive and honest without pushing her away? Should I just keep my mouth shut?*

Introspective Twentysomething, Springfield, MA

A: This is an important juncture, and I appreciate your reaching out. At some point in life, we get to the stage where we realize we may not approve of the people our friends date or marry or have children with. At first you think their partner might grow on you: be kinder, ask you questions, get a haircut, become smart, ski less, wear socks. But then they don't. And once you know you can't change who they are or who your friend loves, there is only one course of action: don't disparage the partner, and keep on being a good friend. Saying something mean about the partner will definitely erode your friend's trust in you, and she'll stop confiding in you out of fear of your judgment. Even if your friend breaks up with this guy, try to refrain from negative comments, as they may get back together. There's nothing worse than hanging out with your friend and her beau after you've called him a "tool" and a "piece of sh*t" while they were on hiatus, a tidbit she likely shared with him. You've mentioned that the relationship is toxic, and I don't take that lightly. I do think there are ways to be honest and supportive while not alienating your friend. If her venting is about needing an audience, and you are up for it emotionally, you could try this: reassure her that you love her and that the situation sounds hard, that you're here to listen. You could also ask questions: *Is there something better he could have said in that moment?* Or make observations: *That sounds like it made you anxious.* Instead of offering a course of action, you're essentially being present, which might allow your friend to do some self-exploration and reflection. I want to add that there's a certain amount of chaos adjacent to toxic dynamics, and it's easy to get sucked into the emotional turmoil and drama. Please know that you are allowed to have boundaries. They're hard to ask for but absolutely crucial to one's sanity. It's OK to say, *I love you and I also think you need to find a therapist to talk to.* Or, *I can go on a walk (or to a movie or shopping) to help you stop thinking about him, but I can't talk about it right now.* I'm really sorry you're going through this. Sadly, this is probably not the last time a person you care about deserves better. But to have someone rooting for us is why we have friends.

Illustration by Kristian Hammerstad

Q: *Whenever I learn someone's address, even from something as benign as sending a postcard to a college friend, I get this urge to look up their home's value on Zillow. Why do I do this? Is my craving to know someone's home value a sign of something bad?*

George C.
Joplin, MO

A: Your looking up people's home values on Zillow *is* a sign of something bad, and it's that you're not using Redfin, which has a much better interface. OK, in all seriousness, you shouldn't feel bad. Let's zoom out. Or should I say Zoom out. (I hate myself right now.) Not to make assumptions, but since you're writing to *The Believer* for advice as opposed to consulting with your favorite TikTok personality, I assume you've lived in a time before social media; my point being—and it's why I made the dumb Zoom joke—that our digital lives are both confusing and unavoidable. And I think there's actually greater disorientation for those of us whose lives weren't always mediated by screens. One tiny speck of the current existential horror, Horror, HORROR (how is this word not big enough anymore?) is occupied by the deluge of social comparison. We're inundated with how everyone else is living. Even more aggravating is that social media is the Russian nesting doll of language and discourse and thus a black hole of concepts and thoughts: it's a meta-tautological Gertrude Stein–M. C. Escher college dorm poster good-dog Gatorade funlick. Like, who can figure this out? Basically, only on the internet could you start going down a social comparison wormhole and end up comparing comparisons, until, by comparison, looking up home values on Zillow becomes the least of your worries. All this is to say, George, that you may not have any control over what you're doing. If I can offer any advice, I would suggest reframing your Zillow habit as curiosity, a trait that should be nurtured, then find a more edifying place for it.

Q: *All my oldest friends come from the community of musicians I grew up in, but I recently entered grad school in a different field. The thing is, I think grad school is making me into a boring person. I've developed some academic interests that are intensely lame to most people, and I can feel my new pursuits putting distance between me and my musician friends. Whenever I see them, I become painfully aware of how non-conversant I've become on the topics that used to unite us. How can I avoid growing apart from my old community?*

John W.
Palo Alto, CA

A: I, too, am part of a community of musicians. I formed a band during my junior year of college that I still play in to this very day. So I relate to the camaraderie of which you speak, and to why it might be scary to pivot from a creative network from which you've derived comfort and inspiration. Moreover, it's never easy to feel your path diverge from a group of friends; no one wants to lose touch, particularly when you've spent years accumulating an encyclopedic knowledge of bands, songs, tour-bus mishaps, former concert venues in your city that are now ice cream shops, and Gibson SGs that only a handful of people—*your* people—truly appreciate and understand. Yet while connecting with others over mutual interests is gratifying, constructing a social currency around the niche and esoteric can be limiting. I once played a game of charades with fellow musicians wherein someone put "The bass player from Neu!" as a clue. That same musician was incensed when no one correctly guessed the answer. They also admonished anyone in the room who possessed only a cursory knowledge of Krautrock. My point being, are you sure *you're* the boring one? It's not what we talk about that makes us boring; it's how. It's knowing when we need to translate our rarefied knowledge so that we're engaging in a conversation, not a lecture. A lecture, for instance, about experimental music from Germany. Or perhaps you're worried that your musician friends are feeling a tad threatened or hurt by the fact that you're thriving outside their insular world. To be honest, maybe they are. But if they're really your friends, I think they'll be supportive of your going to grad school. And I honestly think it might be good for them to branch out. Ultimately, the first step is for you realize that all friendships change as we grow older. If music is what helped you find yourself, your voice, your community, then it will always hold a special place for you. No matter where you end up, you'll never lose the ability to connect with people over music's sacredness, how it jolts and lifts you, floors you, wrecks you—how it finds you. So try not to think of yourself as leaving your community but rather expanding it. Last, if you do nothing else, please familiarize yourself with Neu's bass player. ★

SACRIFICE ZONE

A SEMI-REGULAR GUEST COLUMN ABOUT REGULARLY
IGNORED PLACES. IN THIS ISSUE: EAGLE FORD SHALE

by Deb Olin Unferth

Eagle Ford Shale, *a stretch
of fracking and gas extraction
infrastructure that you could
drive through all day*

L eave the spill and spread of Austin, now the tenth-biggest city in the country, and enter the vast space of rural Texas, fabled for its guns and space rockets. Take State Highway 123 south until it narrows into a thin two-lane road with a sporadic seventy-five-mile-per-hour speed limit and strings of teetering 18-wheelers. Pass the Bender Exotic Game Ranch (now defunct, but where I once spotted a zebra trying to get around the barbed wire). By then you'll be coasting over the Eagle Ford Shale, a sedimentary rock formation first drilled in 2008 and that has since yielded 3.6 billion barrels of oil. Eagle Ford Shale is approximately fifty miles wide and four hundred miles long, a stretch of fracking and gas extraction

Photos throughout by Carol M. Highsmith (Library of Congress, Prints & Photographs Division)

infrastructure that you could drive through all day: oil pads, power plants, pumping stations, pipelines, wastewater disposal wells, processing plants, refineries, compression stations—all the ordnance of a war being waged against the earth, air, water, and life.

Life: There are four maximum-security state prisons tucked into this production/destruction zone. Of the hundred state penitentiaries in Texas, 70 percent are partly or fully un-air-conditioned in the housing areas, including these four prisons. If you look at the map of the Eagle Ford Shale on the Texas.gov Railroad Commission website and find the spot in southeast Texas where the dots—each representing a drilling well—are so dense you can't even read the name of the county underneath, you've found the location of the prison where I've directed a small creative-writing program since 2015. My students and their cellmates wait out their long sentences amid a mess of fossil-fuel pipelines and drilling wells, literally trapped in giant hot boxes of concrete, steel, and razor wire in climate change–era Texas heat, where, without air-conditioning, they could quite possibly bake to death.

The landscape here is already a replacement. These prickly bushes are not thousand-year-old creosote. This area was part of the great savanna grasslands that for millennia covered large parts of the southeastern United States. Tall grasses and widely spaced trees soaked in the rain and supported an array of birds, bison, frogs, and hundreds of animals of the Coastal Plain Floristic Province. In Texas, the savanna mostly disappeared a century ago, after a few dozen years of cattle overgrazing and fire suppression. Now it is sticky brushland, spiny plants, and mesquite trees that don't capture the rain—a completely different ecosystem, drier and harsher.

Then the fracking and extraction began—only fifteen years ago—and the plundering turned catastrophic, biblical: habitats systematically cleared, water tables draining. And flaring: we suck oil out of the ground and burn the parts we don't want, spewing black carbon soot, heavy metals, and sulfur oxides that travel on the wind. At night, in the distance, you can see the flares around Eagle Ford, a hot glow and a low roar on the horizon that make me think of hell.

Perhaps the most bizarre of the oil industry's eccentricities are wastewater

injection wells. Fracking uses massive amounts of water treated with chemicals and combined with sand. The water comes back out, used and polluted, and must be put somewhere. Companies drill special wells, take that used water, and shoot it back into the ground, creating submerged toxic-waste pits that could find their way into the groundwater. It also causes *earthquakes*. We are literally injecting streams of poison into the earth with such force that we are destabilizing existing faults under our feet, breaking the earth's crust in our mad rush to get more oil, *more, more, more.*

Of course, there is little incentive to change, considering all the jobs involved, between the workers and the executives and how they all have to eat and sleep and drink. Besides, are we ready to give up flying?

"Clean energy" poses its own problems. Texas produces the most solar power in the nation after California. But large solar fields are a disaster for the environment. They require ground completely cleared of vegetation: tens of thousands of acres of habitat razed, leaving a chilling, creepy monocrop of metal that will wear out in thirty years and become landfill. I

think it won't be long before all that's left of this land, which until recently was a biodiverse, thriving-animal savanna, will be a poisoned, dried-out carcass strewn with machinery, trucks, contaminated garbage, and incarcerated people gasping in the heat, or dying as they wait for their sentences to end.

Humanity's error seems to me to be ownership, that we believe everything is *ours*—the ground and what's under it, the air and the water and any life residing in them. We are witnessing the slow winding down, the consequences of this error, who and what are being sacrificed.

If you drive a little farther, take a few turns, leave the highway, and go down one small road and then another, you'll begin to feel far from the wreckage. Eventually you'll arrive at Barnhart Q5 Ranch, a seven-hundred-acre nature retreat. It's run by Claire Barnhart and Wilfred Korth, a retired chief ranger with the Guadalupe-Blanco River Authority. They are nurturing the brushland, the grasses, the wildflowers, the cacti, and the thorny brush. You can stay in an Airbnb on the property and photograph the neotropical birds that, due to climate change, are moving into the area. You can wander the ranch trails. I've stayed at this oasis several times while doing longer stints at the prison. In the evenings, I've walked up to the stargazing platform to watch the sunset all around me. At night, in one direction in the distance, you can see the dim hint of the industrial glow of flaring. The sound is just barely audible under the chorus of crickets singing their ancient songs. ⭐

WHAT HENRY JAMES HAS DONE FOR ME

A TEN-YEAR QUEST, FROM MEMPHIS TO THE POCONOS, TO ACQUIRE ALL
TWENTY-SIX VOLUMES OF THE NEW YORK EDITION OF HENRY JAMES

by Ken Howe

My first job in New York was close enough to the Strand to drop by on my lunch hour. One day I came back to work pleased with myself, having found the last books I needed to complete the New York Edition of Henry James—the two volumes of *The Ambassadors*. The pleasure must have shown on my face, because it immediately caught the attention of my colleague George, whose wily old eyes followed me with increasing suspicion as I set down the books, put on my white coat, and sat at the workstation next to him.

"What's got you so happy?" he said in his light Southern growl.

Now in his eighties, George had emeritus status in our department, and saw a light schedule of patients every Wednesday afternoon. These were mostly women of a certain age, who cabbed down from the Upper East Side and looked impossibly elegant walking the institutional corridors of the clinic. Our hospital wasn't really big enough or distinguished enough to have emeriti, but we'd made George one because no other institution would. A lot of people still hated George, and the honors he expected after a long and distinguished career in academic dermatology (which included chairing two major departments) had been denied him. Each year my boss put him up for the Academy's Lifetime Achievement Award, assembling a thick dossier of publications and letters of support to accompany the nomination, and each year someone on the committee blackballed him. In his prime, George had been notorious for subjecting residents and fellows to public humiliation. Those who'd witnessed him in action recalled it with a shudder, even decades later: *He was just vicious. It was really unnecessary.* And now those residents and fellows were chairs themselves. George had trained them well.

I never saw the malevolent, vindictive side of George. And that's an understatement. Rather than getting grilled on differential diagnoses in front of a packed auditorium, or dismissed with annihilating contempt when my answers came up short, I got back rubs. If George found me sitting alone at the workstation, he'd come up behind, drop a big hand on

each of my shoulders, and give a surprisingly powerful squeeze. George's clawlike hands still had a lot of grip in them. These massages never went on for long. I'd squirm away, he'd laugh, and we'd both get back to work. But the old stories of George dominating grand rounds with his relentless bullying were not hard for me to believe. A hint of the same aggressive energy persisted in the attention I received from him, harmless as it was.

When I asked about George, an older dermatologist who'd trained under him said, "He's clearly gay, but I don't think he's ever—there's never been anyone, that I know of. Nothing open, at least. George has always been a 'confirmed bachelor'"—the dermatologist waggled his fingers to indicate scare quotes—"which was the only option in those days, if you wanted to chair a department."

In conversation George often maintained eye contact a beat longer than normal, which had the effect of putting an unspoken question in the air. But the day I returned from the Strand, his eyes were darting all over me, trying to figure out what I'd been doing. "What's got you so pleased? What've you been up to?"

"I went to the Strand during lunch."

The teasing look dropped from his face. His eyes went dead. Only then did he notice the yellow bag on the desk. "That what you got?"

Illustration by Pete Gamlen

I nodded.

"Show me." I pulled out one of the volumes and handed it to him. He looked at the cover. He didn't open it. "Henry James," he read, then slowly shook his head, a sardonic smile forming on his lips. "Is this what you run out on your lunch hour to do? This is what you want to get out of life?"

The answers to George's questions were yes and yes, but I couldn't say that to him. I knew how he'd react, and I didn't want to hear it. George was always after me to publish in the big derm journals, submit my name for junior positions on Academy committees. And while I was willing to accept his mentorship within the field of dermatology, what I did with my life outside that—well, let's just say George didn't strike me as a good example to emulate. I figured I could do a lot better on my own.

DESSERTS EATEN BY LOURDES IN *DREAMING IN CUBAN*

✶ Pecan sticky buns
✶ Honey buns
✶ Coconut ice cream
✶ Strawberry shortcake
✶ Chocolate éclairs
✶ Apple pies
✶ Arroz con leche
✶ Shortbread cookies
✶ Capuchinos
✶ Cuban churros

—*list compiled by Joanna Buoniconti*

About a decade earlier, when I was still a medical student, I'd found thirteen of the twenty-six volumes of the New York Edition of Henry James. They were in a cardboard box on the sidewalk outside a bookdealer's shop in West LA. The dealer came hurrying out when he saw me looking at them.

"That's a broken set," he said right away. "They're not all there."

"I understand," I said, still kneeling over them.

Asked about price, he named such an impossibly low figure—I think it was ten bucks—that I wanted to snatch up the box immediately; but before I could, he said they were for sale under one condition: that I never try to complete the set.

"Because you won't be able to do it! You'll drive yourself crazy looking! Don't even try!"

He was like the guy in an old movie who staggers out of the desert, utters these fateful words, and dies. I'm sure he meant well, but I didn't think I needed his advice—from what I could see, there didn't seem enough overlap between our lives for it to apply.

"Promise me you won't do it," he insisted.

I tried to laugh off his warning.

"I'm serious! I'm not letting you have these if you don't promise."

I have made three public pledges in my life: the Hippocratic oath, my wedding vows, and this one, the promise I made to this desperate, broken man, standing on the sidewalk of Westwood Boulevard.

I promised: "I won't look for them."

"OK," said the man, visibly relieved. And let me take the box.

As I drove away in my secondhand Tercel, the box of books riding alongside me in the passenger seat, my heart began pumping with dark joy. Because I *would* find the rest of those books. I knew I would. If the world was one enormous shelf, somewhere along its length—it might be at mile two or mile two thousand—were the books I was looking for. They were out there, and I was coming for them.

In the end it took me ten years—nearly a third of my life at the time. Our lives are meaningless without desires, and for a decade I had the good fortune to live a life replete with meaning. Every bookshelf I came across put me under a kind of spell, while my eyes scanned for the telltale spines: black, with a gilt-edged blue band, or if they still had dust jackets (highly preferable), a distinctive, elegant blue-gray, the color of a smoky Venetian dusk. Most of the thirteen were found in used-book stores, but I discovered one at a public library sale in Memphis, Tennessee, and came across several more—they were volumes I already had, alas—at a yard sale in the Poconos. I even spotted a set on a White House tour. The set was complete, but lacked dust jackets. Security was too tight to risk snatching a volume.

The Novels and Tales of Henry James, New York Edition presents the works of the Master that he chose to preserve for posterity in a deluxe, uniform edition. In it, James collected (and recollected) himself. Scribner's offered to publish a complete works in thirty-five volumes, but James insisted on limiting it to a selection. According to biographer Leon Edel, the number of volumes he originally fixed upon for the New York Edition—twenty-three[1]—held special significance for James, but he had miscalculated and could no longer squeeze all the material into that size. The twenty-four volumes of the 1907–09 first edition—followed by two posthumous volumes in 1919—contain the famous prefaces, written specifically for the edition, in which James sets down his thoughts on the art of fiction. In several cases the donnée, or germ, of his most famous stories is disclosed as well.

To be clear, my collection is not an original 1907–09 set, with photogravure frontispieces by Alvin Langdon Coburn, but the uniform reprint edition put out by Scribner's in the '60s. I did come across a complete first-edition set once, in the kind of antiquarian shop—Oriental rugs, polished library tables, busts of Dante and Cicero—that doesn't put prices in its books. But I wouldn't spend that much on Henry James even if I could afford to. What would be the point? It'd just spoil the fun.

Same thing with the internet. Nowadays, thirty minutes on Bookfinder, Amazon, and eBay is all you need to complete even the most broken set of the New York Edition. Then it's just a matter of waiting for packages to arrive. You'll get the books you want, but you'll pay a premium, and not only in terms of price. Immediate gratification achieves the former at the expense of the latter. The pre-internet way of searching for a find—hunting through used-book stores, crouching among the mildew and dust—wasn't efficient, but it served a purpose. All that time spent looking kindled desire. It made the book you wanted seem even more precious. All those afternoons when I found nothing—and that I regarded as futile and wasted—were in fact forging value, as with each passing hour, with every scanned shelf, the sought-for titles grew more desirable in my mind.

And then when I actually found one, I couldn't believe my eyes. That's what happened during my lunch hour that day at the Strand. I wasn't expecting anything, just popped into the "J" aisle as part of my usual rounds, and there they were: volumes 21 and 22, *The Ambassadors*, in beautiful "near fine" condition, unmarked except for the burnished patina unhandled books acquire with the passage of thirty tranquil years. A wondering sense of disbelief swept over me as I pulled them from the shelf; even held in my hands, they didn't seem quite real. And of my feet carrying me to the checkout counter, or floating up Broadway to return to work, I have no memory.

---

1. This is Leon Edel's idea, and I don't know how accepted it is by other scholars. He writes: "The choice of 23 volumes was thus not arbitrary. There seems to have been a special reason for it. The figure seems indeed to have had a certain magical quality for James; when he needs a date, a youthful age, a general number, he often fixes on 23." Edel then quotes a bit of dialogue from *The Awkward Age:* "I see you go in for sets… *big* sets. What's this— 'Vol 23 *The British Poets.*' Vol 23 is delightful—do tell me about Vol 23." Edel goes on to some psychological speculation—that James was always the third person in relations with his mother and brother, that his aunt Kate was the third person in his parents' marriage. "Triangular relations are at the heart of his novels." Finally Edel notes that Balzac's complete works came out in 23 volumes, a numerical fact noted by James in his first essay on Balzac, the novelist James considered "the father of us all."

MICROINTERVIEW WITH NOOR NAGA, PART II

THE BELIEVER: You've talked about the difficulties of writing in the voice of a character who is so far from your personal experience. Your response was to embrace the "wrongness" of it. Do you think it's important for writers to confront their limitations within their work?

NOOR NAGA: Well, I think what you're asking about is the distance between the writer and the characters they're embodying, and to what extent that distance can be collapsed. I think you can do it if you cultivate a kind of listening. If you're willing to move through the everyday, in your imagination, of a particular character, then it's a bit like Method acting. You just have to really get inside of it and commit to being there in the mundane. You have to think about things like: How does this character walk across a room? How do they pull something out of a fridge? Very small, granular details like that. And if you take the time to do that, then I don't think there are many characters that are inaccessible to you. It just takes patience and commitment to the bit, especially the boring parts of the bit. Very similar to Method acting. ✷

For a collector, a great find always makes life feel, for the moment, like a dream. You cannot believe your luck. Suddenly the everyday world isn't big enough to contain your happiness. The expanding joy crowds out everything else. In those moments, there is only the dream.

Of course, this state of affairs can't go on forever. Something always wakes you up. For me that day in the clinic, it was George.

In our year of working together, it had occurred to me more than once that George was a bit of a Jamesian character himself. There was the same crepuscular fondness of the aging-but-still-feeling man for the unformed, promising youth (that would be me). But unlike the original ambassador, Lambert Strether, George never said, "Live all you can; it's a mistake not to"—he didn't even read those words, though he could have that day in the clinic. All he had to do was open to page 217. But an outburst like Strether's—summoned through the deep and difficult work of reckoning with one's life experience—wasn't really George's style. Whatever "reaction against the mistake" he might have felt was not a matter he was willing to disclose—not to me, anyway.

"I want you to tell me something," he said, gazing pensively at the book in his hands.

"All right," I said.

He didn't continue right away, though I could see he was about to. Something was on his mind. The little muscles at the corners of his mouth were working while he thought out the best way to put it. Speaking slowly, snapping out each word like a cardsharp laying down a winning hand, he said: "What has Henry James ever done for you?"

He raised a bristly gray eyebrow in quivering triumph.

"Think about it," he said, and tossed the book at me.

For a terrifying instant the book bounced around in my juggling grasp, until I managed to grab hold of it and, with shaking hands, restore it to the safety of the bag. When I looked up, George was watching me. The question he had asked still hung in the air, but I just smiled and gave no answer. George nodded, having expected as much. To him, there *was* no answer to his question—only the obvious "nothing." The question was meant to be a trap, and he'd sprung it perfectly.

In 1907, when Henry James received the first volume of the New York Edition from his publishers, he wrote back to them, "The whole is a perfect felicity, so let us go on rejoicing." And that's pretty much what I had done for those ten happy years: rejoiced from one store to another, one book to the next. And now the whole was complete. That evening I would slide the final volumes into their place on the shelf.

I could have tried explaining this to George, but I didn't think he would get it. Whatever I had to say for myself would be overcome by his innate hostility. Like many people (*most* people, actually), he thought my time would be far better spent playing tennis, or networking to further my career—anything but combing through used-book stores in search of some grimy tome. But we can't always expect our pleasures to be understood. That's asking too much of them. It's enough that they please *us*. We live the way we can, and take what joy we're given. It's a mistake not to. And while he would never say so, I had the feeling that on some level George understood this too. ✶

MICROINTERVIEW WITH NOOR NAGA, PART III

THE BELIEVER: The characters in your novel dream of many things at night: tangerines, Kendrick Lamar, cigarettes, pomegranate seeds. Do you keep a record of your dreams?

NOOR NAGA: I don't keep an official record, but I dream extensively every night, and I spend a lot of time thinking about the patterns of themes. I have a very obvious subconscious. Anything I'm stressed about, I will see manifested as a nightmare. I spend a lot of time paying attention to what my subconscious is telling me and trying to bring to the surface those things I'm suppressing. I dream of my family every single night, my cousins and my siblings and my parents and my grandmother, which is a bit strange. I don't dream of my friends almost ever. I think that says a lot. ✶

ODD BIRD

by Teddy Goldenberg

26

GENE LUEN YANG

[GRAPHIC NOVELIST]

"THE FOUNDATION OF THESE STORIES THAT I LOVE, THAT I GREW UP WITH AND THAT FORMED MY CONSCIENCE AND MY CONSCIOUSNESS—THEY'RE ROOTED IN SOMETHING THAT'S VERY ANTI-ME."

What Gene Luen Yang relies on to ease the challenges of comics-making:
Handwriting fonts
A portable drawing tablet
The camaraderie of fellow cartoonists

Cartoonist Gene Luen Yang is having a good year. His most beloved masterpiece, American Born Chinese, *which began as a xeroxed and stapled series hand-sold at comics conventions and became the first graphic novel finalist for the National Book Award, is now, seventeen years after its release, debuting as a Disney+ TV show starring Oscar winners Michelle Yeoh and Ke Huy Quan.*

American Born Chinese *has been a staple of my syllabus in almost every comics class I've taught. It's the graphic novel that teaches the lesson of form: the best comics do things that only comics can do. ABC's formal innovation, most notably the satirical use of stereotypes to skewer the white American gaze, explores the tensions of assimilation and the paradoxes of identity experienced by so many immigrant groups in America. But true comics obsessives (like me) know that Yang's oeuvre exceeds* ABC, *and it's epically vast: his first books, self-published under the imprint Humble*

Illustration by Kristian Hammerstad

Comics, won him a Xeric Foundation grant in 1997. Prime Baby *(2010);* Boxers and Saints *(2013);* Dragon Hoops *(2020); the collaborative works* The Eternal Smile *(2009),* Level Up *(2011),* Secret Coders *(2015-18), and others; along with his writing for* Avatar: The Last Airbender, Superman, *his most recent* Books of Clash, *and other superhero and adventure comics, all build a legacy that delights in variations on nerdery and everyday heroism. Yang is a MacArthur Fellow, a recipient of the Michael L. Printz Award, a National Ambassador for Young People's Literature, and a many-time Eisner and Harvey Award winner.*

Given these accomplishments, it's hard not to dwell on how humble he remains. Yang, now fifty, taught high school computer science for seventeen years, and he has four children of his own. Born and bred in California, he often cites his OG Bay Area cartoonist community as an essential influence. He lives in the town where his parents—an electrical engineer from Taiwan and a programmer who grew up in Taiwan and Hong Kong—first met, and he's finishing a rom-com graphic novel, a collaboration with illustrator and writer LeUyen Pham, loosely based on his and his wife's love story. Yang's is a rare voice in this century's literary world: he is a deeply moral storyteller who doesn't moralize. His work is often radical in its compassion. He refuses to create villains for the sake of others' heroism.

Between trips to the White House and Radio City Music Hall, Yang spent some time with me over Zoom this past summer. He asked me almost as many questions as I asked him, and when I challenged him to define "the good," he didn't even flinch.

—*Amy Kurzweil*

I. THE SUFFERING

THE BELIEVER: So you're having a whirlwind time lately.

GENE LUEN YANG: It's been really, really weird. A little bit whiplashy.

BLVR: Well, I'm just a straight-up comics nerd, so this will be a very comics-specific conversation.

GLY: OK. My favorite.

BLVR: So I was recently reading *Loyola Chin and the San Peligran Order*—

GLY: Oh my gosh, you went deep. There are, like, five copies of that somewhere!

BLVR: Your postscript in that book struck me. You wrote about the physicality of making comics and the question of whether or not all the labor is worth it. I just finished my second graphic memoir—368 pages, seven years—and it almost killed me, physically. Can you tell me about your relationship to the physical aspect of comics-making?

GLY: My cartoonist friends and I always talk about our crappy cartoonist bodies. It's a stereotype, but I feel like a lot of us are not physical specimens. [*Laughs*] And maybe that's what drew us to comics in the first place. Almost all of us have something that hurts. Usually for me it's my shoulders and back.

American Born Chinese took me five years to finish. And during those five years, I had no idea how the book was going to turn out, if I was going to actually like it by the end. So there's just a lot of suffering. There's suffering on one side, and then there's an unknown result on the other. I think a lot of us in comics struggle with that.

BLVR: How do you deal with the suffering and uncertainty of this kind of work?

GLY: Technology does help. Like there was this argument about hand-lettering when I was starting in comics in the '90s.

BLVR: I find that's actually the most painful part of comics.

GLY: I do think hand-lettering is more beautiful. And you can move your text between words and pictures. Will Eisner does that a lot. But the compromise most of us have made is that we use a font that's based on our handwriting.

BLVR: Yeah, I have four different fonts.

GLY: I do too. And it's imperfect. But that's part of the way I deal with the suffering. The other thing is community. I think cartooning can be very lonely work. But I do have a group of friends who are also cartoonists, and I think my friendship with them is actually one of the big benefits of doing comics. Possibly, like, the best benefit.

BLVR: Do you have text threads going throughout your workday where you're sharing pictures of your drawings with these friends?

GLY: Yeah. Right now I'm collaborating on a graphic novel called *Lunar New Year Love Story* with LeUyen Pham. I did the writing and she did the art, although it kind of bleeds. We're constantly texting each other.

BLVR: You mentioned technology. Can you tell me about your tools? Are there parts of the process that you still like to do by hand?

GLY: The most recent graphic novel that I wrote and drew, *Dragon Hoops*, was the very first time that I drew completely digitally, and I did it mostly on a Wacom tablet. I didn't use any paper at all. Before that, for *American Born Chinese* and for *Boxers and Saints* and for the comics that only you've read—

BLVR: [*Laughs*]

GLY: —I used actual paper with actual ink.

BLVR: What kind of ink?

GLY: I don't remember the brand—it's been so long—but it was india ink. And then I had a sable brush. I think I started with the number four, which was a really bad idea. I got it because it was on sale.

BLVR: Yeah, that's really thick.

GLY: Too big. I think I was using a number one by the end. I did *American Born Chinese* like that. And then with *Boxers and Saints*, I moved to these Japanese brush pens. Pentel makes one that I really like.

BLVR: That's my pen: the Pentel.

GLY: Wait, so you're still drawing on paper?

BLVR: Yeah, unfortunately.

GLY: That's awesome.

BLVR: Is it?

GLY: Do you want to move to digital?

BLVR: Well, it has not come to me naturally, but it does seem faster. How did you make that transition?

GLY: The main thing is you have to resist the temptation to zoom in. Because you can just zoom in forever and fix things on a pixel level.

BLVR: So you've given yourself arbitrary constraints?

GLY: Arbitrary constraints. That's right. But I don't think I'm necessarily faster digitally. I'm more portable. That's the most important thing.

BLVR: Because you're on the road, going to the White House…

GLY: Well, there has been that this past month. But this past month is not my normal life. No, I have to be portable because my wife and I have four kids. And we live in a four-bedroom house. And I used to have an office, but then one of my daughters got too big to share with her sisters. So she got my office room. Now I'm a nomad.

II. PAC-MAN AND COLONOSCOPIES

BLVR: I've noticed that video games are a theme in your work. Right now you're doing *Books of Clash*, which is an adaptation of a video game into a comic. And you've got *Level Up*, illustrated by Thien Pham, which also features elements drawn from video games. What do games mean to you?

GLY: I'm not a video game player anymore, but I was when I was a kid. I'm gonna sound like an old person now, but when things went 3-D, I had a hard time transitioning. I would feel carsick. But when stuff was 2-D, I really loved it—like *Pac-Man* and *Super Mario Bros.*, all of that. When I was in college, my roommates and I were really into *NBA Jam* and *Bomberman*. And then things went 3-D and I had a harder time with it.

BLVR: Comics are like 2-D games, right? What is it about more simplistic games that appeals to you?

GLY: 2-D games, like cartoons, are a simplified version of reality. But once you get into 3-D, they're trying to get to reality, or as close to reality as possible.

BLVR: Have you ever put on the Oculus and gone into VR and all that?

GLY: I've tried a little bit. It's kind of cool. But I'm also freaked out about it.

BLVR: I feel there's two schools of thought here. One is the people who feel there's more elegance and artistry in a simplified world—people who are trying to pare things down in order to say something. And then there are people who are trying to really immerse you in a sensory experience. And sometimes in that direction, you're having so much of a sensory experience that you can't have a conceptual experience. Something that I really like about your style is that its simplicity allows for it to be especially conceptual.

GLY: That's a great way of talking about it.

BLVR: Have you read this book called *Games: Agency as Art* by C. Thi Nguyen?

GLY: No, should I? I'm gonna write it down.

BLVR: He's a philosopher of games. His thesis is that games are an art form and their medium is agency.

GLY: I think that's very true. Like in *Level Up*, we were trying to use games as a way of talking about control. And I think that was the appeal, at least for me when I was a kid. *Pac-Man* or *Donkey Kong* was one of the few places where I got to make all the decisions. There's no parent figure within those worlds that tells you what to do.

BLVR: Do you think there's a relationship between kids who are into video games and kids who lack control in other places? Were your parents telling you what to do all the time?

GLY: Oh, of course. I think that's true of a lot of parents in general, but immigrant parents in particular, because they work so hard to establish this life for you. They don't want

you to mess it up. For me, that was more my dad than my mom. My mom was more understanding. My mom, I think, had an artist's heart. But my dad was very much a stereotypical immigrant dad, at least in what he wanted from me and my brother.

BLVR: What was the family dynamic? Did both you and your brother feel the pressure from your father to, like the *Level Up* character, become a doctor or something?

GLY: The *Level Up* character is loosely based on my brother. My brother is a doctor. He's four years younger than me and he was always better at video games than me. He just had better hand-eye coordination. I remember him telling me all these crazy stories about the stuff he would have to do in med school, like dissecting human cadavers and labeling hemisected human heads. The way video games and medicine connected for me was him telling me that for one of his assignments, he had to do a colonoscopy on somebody. And after that, he decided to be a gastroenterologist. When he was a kid, he was super squeamish. So I was like, "You used to feel like throwing up when you saw dog poop on the street. Why would you want to be a gastroenterologist?" And he said, "Because a colonoscopy is like playing video games up somebody's ass."

BLVR: [*Laughs*]

GLY: I was like, "That's a graphic novel."

III. TAKING ADVANTAGE OF THE FORM

BLVR: The big thing in your life right now is that *American Born Chinese* has been adapted as a television show, and I'm especially interested in what it's like for that particular work to traverse mediums. *American Born Chinese* is one of the most formally innovative comics maybe ever.

GLY: Well, thank you. That's so nice of you to say.

BLVR: There's so many comics-specific choices you're making. How do those choices get adapted, or not, into a form like television? For example, the fact that we never see Jin's parents' faces in the book. Are people in TV noticing those choices and saying, *OK, we noticed that we never see*

Jin's parents' faces. What does that mean for the story and how we adapt it?

GLY: So the short answer is: the TV show is very different. In my first conversations with Melvin Mar, one of the executive producers on the show, and Kelvin Yu, the showrunner, we emphasized that the story had to take advantage of the medium. When you tell a story, you have to be conscious of the strengths and the weaknesses of the medium you're using. And because I'm a comics guy, when I do comics I often try to do things that you can only do in comics. I think that's an ethos that comes from the crew of cartoonists I came up with when I was in my twenties. For that specific thing you mentioned about the parents, the show makes the opposite choice. The parents are actually these big characters in the show. But in the book I think you only see, like, half their faces on one page.

We made two choices very early on. One was to adapt it as a television series instead of a movie, which meant the world had to feel more full. It had to feel open-ended. And two was to move the timeline from the vague '80s/'90s, when the book was set, which mirrors my own childhood, to now, the 2020s. So lots of stuff has to change because of those two choices. And I actually like that the show is very different from the book, because I'm hoping that the negative space between the show and the book says something.

BLVR: What do you want that negative space to say?

GLY: That the experience of being an Asian American is very different now from when I was growing up. That's one. And then two is the difference between the mediums. I think going through this experience with Hollywood has just emphasized for me how intimate comics is. Comics is a much, much more intimate medium than television. Television is amazing. And it's an intensely collaborative medium. But I think there are certain stories and ways of telling stories that you can only do through comics.

BLVR: Are there intimate moments from the book that you do see reflected in the television show?

GLY: One of the central pieces of the book is the friendship between Jin and Wei-Chen, the American-born Chinese kid and the foreign exchange student, and I think that was preserved and maybe even expressed better in the show because of the two actors [Ben Wang and Jimmy Liu]. And you also get more time with them. You can read the graphic novel in, what, forty-five minutes? It took me five years to make, but you can read it in forty-five minutes.

BLVR: Ugh. The worst.

GLY: But that's fine. [*Laughs*]

BLVR: Television is real time and the characters are like friends. I think that's the primary way people relate to television. People get to be companioned by Jin and Wei-Chen. But they're not *becoming* Jin and Wei-Chen, which is what it feels like to read *American Born Chinese*. You become Jin even if you're, I don't know, a Jewish girl across the country, fifteen years later.

GLY: Yeah, that's the Scott McCloud idea. The cartoons are avatars for us.

IV. LESSONS IN SATIRE

BLVR: The iconic stereotype in your work is Chin-Kee, the visiting Chinese cousin from the third story line of *American Born Chinese*. And let me shout out one of the most brilliant formal choices in all of comics: the laugh track that accompanies all Chin-Kee's scenes in the book. I've never had a student encounter Chin-Kee as a stereotype and not understand that it is a stereotype used to defang stereotypes, because of that laugh track. How did that choice occur to you?

GLY: Some of it was inspired by my cousins. My cousins came to the United States when they were older, and the way they learned about American culture was through sitcoms. In the '80s, sitcoms were the picture of what an ideal family in America should act like. And there were no Asian characters in those shows.

So it seemed like if you ever inserted Asian-ness into this quintessentially American setting, that somebody would find it funny.

BLVR: The minority characters are the punch lines to these shows.

GLY: If they exist, they are the punch lines.

BLVR: Did some people not get the nuance of the Chin-Kee character? I know there was some controversy with the character getting taken out of context on the internet. Was that a serious episode in your writing life?

GLY: There were some people who misunderstood, but the vast majority did not. So *American Born Chinese* began as a mini comic. I would write and draw it, xerox it at Kinko's, staple it, and then sell it by hand. At the end of the day, I would sell maybe sixteen copies. I knew most of the people who bought it. I would trade it with other cartoonists, you know. So in that context, I didn't think anybody would misread him. After the book came out in 2006, I'd say I had three major responses to that character. One is that sometimes older Asian Americans would tell me they found Chin-Kee so painful that they had a hard time finishing the book. Which I think is fine. He's supposed to be painful. A second response I would get is people would find him funny, but they would feel uncomfortable laughing. And I think that's fine too. Because he's supposed to be absurd to the point of being funny. And then there was this final response where people would come up to me at, like, a Comic Con—and this was definitely a minority response; I haven't had this in a long time—but they'd be like, "You know that cousin character—he's so cute. Do you have a T-shirt with him on it?"

BLVR: Wow.

GLY: And that would make me feel very uncomfortable. They completely missed what I was trying to do with that character. But that was definitely the minority. Most people understood what I was trying to do.

BLVR: Did you ever feel pressure to condemn what Chin-Kee skewers in a more didactic way?

GLY: I don't know if I'd call it pressure. For cousin Chin-Kee, specifically, there is some pushback, especially now. And I get some of where that pushback is coming from. I think I can also trace cousin Chin-Kee back to my high school English class, my senior year, when we did this unit on satire and we read Jonathan Swift's *A Modest Proposal*. We had to write response essays, and I wrote one about being a Chinese American. I remember my teacher reading it in class, and she chose to read it at the very end of the period, so she knew she wouldn't be able to finish it, and I remember some of my classmates being uncomfortable with it. I also remember thinking that it was a really powerful way of talking about something. That particular lesson on satire is one of the few things I remember from my senior year of high school. My response to some of the pushback that's happening now is that satire always has the danger of being misunderstood. But if you have a technique that you can't apply to a minority experience, then you reserve it as a writing tool only for the majority. That seems even more dangerous than satire being misunderstood.

BLVR: Satire does imply that we all believe the same thing, that we all understand what's true so we can identify what's untrue. In *American Born Chinese*, Chin-Kee is an illusion; he's a manifestation of the white gaze. But if you're in the white gaze, and you see Chin-Kee as real, you're not going to get the satire.

GLY: That's right. In terms of the pressure, I think there's no question that we have become more sensitive about issues of identity. And I think, on the whole, it's a good thing. It just means that conversations that used to happen under the surface are now happening above the surface. I do think that writers and creators have to be sensitive to where the conversation is now.

V. SARAN WRAP AND OTHER PRESERVATIVES

BLVR: In *American Born Chinese*, in both the show and the book, there's this Jin–and–Wei-Chen dynamic, a tension between a more recent immigrant and a more assimilated character. Is there a Wei-Chen in your life?

GLY: Oh yeah. There are multiple. My parents, for sure. I remember going to the mall with them and just feeling really embarrassed when they spoke Chinese to me, even though we spoke Chinese at home. At the mall, I'd try to talk to them in English, and they would answer in English, but it'd be accented English, and I'd feel even more embarrassed. This was when I was in late elementary school, early junior high. Then there was the kid who came from Taiwan. I must have been in third or fourth grade, and he was a year younger than me. This is a very shameful memory. The teacher kind of assigned him to me, to be his friend. She thought she was doing both of us a favor. And I just felt so embarrassed. This kid—his English wasn't very good. He'd follow me around and speak Chinese to me. Finally, at the end of the week, the way I got him to stop following me around was by throwing tanbark at him. I don't know if you know what tanbark is.

BLVR: No, what is tanbark?

GLY: It's these wood chips they used to line playgrounds with in the '80s. Anyway, in junior high, there were two groups of Asian American boys. Me and my crew, we were mostly born in the United States or came when we were very young. And then there were these other kids that came when they were older, like in fifth or sixth grade. And they were very much like Wei-Chen. They would wear these weird shirts with misspelled English words on them. And they would listen to Asian music and speak to each other in their native tongue. We had this weird frenemy relationship. If we were in class together, we'd say hi to them, we would talk to them. But we always wanted to make sure that people knew we were two distinct groups. And behind their backs, we'd call them FOBs, "fresh off the boats," and make fun of their accents and their clothes.

BLVR: I assume your attitude toward that group has changed. How do you reflect on these memories now?

GLY: My attitude toward them definitely has changed. I feel bad. I feel bad for feeling embarrassed. I think it was just a sign of immaturity. I think it was just wrong.

BLVR: I wonder if you think there was

any part of you that was jealous of them and their access to their culture.

GLY: I've never considered that question before. Maybe in some contexts. But I don't think I felt jealous at school. At school, I wanted to avoid them at all costs. But I did also go to Chinese school on the weekends, and maybe in that context I might have been jealous.

BLVR: In my own family, there's also this kind of FOB dynamic. My grandmother is a Holocaust survivor born in Poland. She has an accent and she does all this embarrassing stuff, acting like a cheap Jew. And we, her family, are the greatest policers of her behavior. But over time, we started to kind of use that embarrassment for humor. Like, we're going to be the first ones to laugh about, and also celebrate, my grandmother. It's a coping strategy but also a source of empowerment. I'm curious if there's a parallel in your family or your culture?

GLY: There's absolutely a parallel. I think immigrants all tell kind of the same stories, and it's a way for us to bond with each other. For example, in the *American Born Chinese* show, most people are not going to notice this, but the television remote control in the very first episode is wrapped in saran wrap, which is totally a very Chinese immigrant thing to do, and then there's a sponge that's in a tofu container next to the kitchen sink. I've done talks about *American Born Chinese* where I show these images in my PowerPoint, and I always get a huge reaction, because people just recognize those things. As a kid, you're embarrassed because you think these things make you different from everybody else. But as an adult, you realize they actually make you the same as a whole bunch of people.

BLVR: With my grandmother, it's putting sheets and towels all over the furniture. And other families put plastic around their furniture. What do you think is underneath that impulse?

GLY: I think it's protection. Protection and preservation, which maybe we take for granted as Americans, because things for us are very replaceable. My brother has a little bit of that too. I hope he doesn't mind me busting him out, but he had this Acura that he kept for seventeen years, and there's this plastic that protects these metal parts of the car floor, and he never took off the plastic. He gave the car to my dad—my nineteen-year-old son borrows it when he's home from college—and my brother is proud of the fact that the plastic is still on there. None of us have ever seen it without the plastic.

BLVR: Do you have these tendencies?

GLY: I probably do. But I bet I can't even see them. Definitely less so than my parents. I think that's the tension between me and them: my approach to the world is much more American in that I think of things as replaceable.

VI. K-SHAPED PROGRESS

BLVR: There's a lot of anxiety about the moral education of young people in the literary world. Something I love about your work is that it's not amoral, but it does feature moral complexity. In *Superman Smashes the Klan*, a character who commits an act of white supremacy is ultimately humanized. The reader understands where he is coming from. Do you ever get pushback against this kind of moral complexity in your work?

GLY: I've had some pushback. With *Superman Smashes the Klan*, it's that it doesn't go hard enough. That character, Chuck, the kid that kind of has a change of heart, I didn't make him up. He's actually from the original '40s radio show [that *Superman Smashes the Klan* is based on]. He has the same arc in the radio show as he does in the book. I think you have to have compassion for all your characters in order to write them properly, even the characters that you disagree with. When I was preparing to write *Superman Smashes the Klan*, I was actually watching a lot of YouTube videos of—what do they call them?—racial realist apologists.

BLVR: What's a racial realist apologist?

GLY: It's somebody who believes that the differences between the races are real and that ultimately a multicultural society is impossible because the races are too different. I was watching this stuff to really try to understand where those characters are coming from. And there's a danger in that, too, right? Because in the end, I really didn't want people to go, *Oh, you know, the guy in the hood had a point.*

BVLR: Right.

GL: My hope is that by the end of the book, the point that Superman and the Lee family make is stronger than the other point. But I also don't want to straw-man the other point, because I think it takes away the power of the narrative.

BLVR: What did you learn about where those kinds of characters are coming from?

GLY: I mean, living in diverse societies is hard. There are studies, cited in those YouTube videos, about how people in diverse societies tend to not be as happy as people in mono-ethnic states. But the future is multicultural. I just don't see a way around that. You can't roll back technology, you can't roll back the cultural exchange that's happened. So if you're future-minded, you have to engage in a multicultural landscape.

BLVR: When you wrote *Superman Smashes the Klan*, were you thinking about Superman's creators and their identities?

GLY: Absolutely. I think Superman is a science fiction version of the Jewish American experience. And I think there's a lot of overlap between the Chinese American and the Jewish American experience. But one of the ways in which they don't overlap is that for some people in some Jewish communities, there is this choice to pass, right?

BLVR: That's right.

GLY: And that's fundamental in Superman: that he can choose to pass when he becomes Clark Kent.

BLVR: Yes. But in *Superman Smashes the Klan*, he's *psychologically* unable to pass. He has these moments where he's overwhelmed by his true alien identity. And what overwhelms him is *memory*.

GLY: That's right, yeah.

BLVR: Going back to the question of moral complexity: I found the horror of *Boxers and Saints*, the constant war and death of that period of history, so surprising in a story for young readers. Have you thought about what it means to write for children, what you can or shouldn't show them, and how to engage with darkness and death?

GLY: There are definitely some really dark children's stories and fairy tales out there. My understanding is that, for example, the Snow White we know in America is not the original Snow White—the original was much darker, with lots of pain and torture. To be honest, especially with *Boxers and Saints* and with *American Born Chinese*, I wasn't totally thinking about age demographics. Age demographics, historically, have not been very important in comics. When I was a kid, in the comic book store, there might have been a kids' section with some *Uncle Scrooge* and stuff. And there was an adult section, which meant *adult* adult. But the vast majority of stuff was in this middle section. And in there you'd have *Spider-Man*, all the versions of *Spider-Man*. And then Peter Bagge's *Hate* would be there; sometimes *Love and Rockets*. It would all just be in this big mass in the middle

So I wasn't really aware of age demographics until I signed with First Second. They categorized me as YA, and I think that fits pretty well. My series *Secret Coders* and my most recent series, *Books of Clash*, are specifically for middle-grade. But for *Boxers and Saints* specifically, the violence was a response to what I was reading, what I was finding in my research. It just seemed so bloody. I went to visit a Jesuit archive in France, where they had all these black-and-white photos from turn-of-the-century China. They had photos of beheadings where the head would actually be halfway between the ground and the body. And if you think about camera technology back then, somebody really wanted that shot in order to get it. That says something about people's mentality back then.

BLVR: They were relishing the violence?

GLY: They must have been. Why else would you choose to do that? If you just wanted evidence that the beheading happened, why wouldn't you snap the shot after the beheading was over? You had to purposely want the head in midair.

BLVR: *Boxers and Saints* must have required spending a lot of time in a pretty bloody world. How long did that take you?

GLY: About five or six years.

BLVR: I've heard you say that you wrote two books because you didn't know who the good guys were in the Boxer Rebellion, so you had to write both sides of the story. Did your sympathies coalesce to one side or the other by the end?

GLY: I don't think they coalesced. I didn't want to write two books. But I couldn't decide who the hero was. And I don't think I've landed on an answer. That's definitely a conflict. I feel very sympathetic to both sides.

BLVR: Did readers come to you with their own conclusions about their sympathies?

GLY: Oh, absolutely. Within religious circles, people are more sympathetic to the Christians. But I think the majority of everybody else is more sympathetic to the Boxers.

BLVR: My own reading of that conflict is that on the one hand, these colonialist characters bring a very racist perspective, and yet they also bring something that gives the Vibiana character, the Christian convert, a real way out of a lot of hardship and suffering. How would you characterize your own reckoning with Christianity and colonialism?

GLY: I grew up in a Chinese Catholic church, and when I was a kid, it seemed like Chinese culture and this Western Catholicism just kind of went hand in hand. It wasn't until I got older that I realized that's not really the case historically, or even in the present day. The history of Christianity is really, really complex. The central figure, to my mind, is very sympathetic. But the ways in which those stories have been lived out have often been pretty heinous. In a lot of ways, the way I feel about the Catholic Church as a Chinese American mirrors the way I feel about America as a Chinese American, which kind of mirrors the way I feel about humanity in general.

BLVR: Can you say more about that? What is the mirroring?

GLY: For both Catholicism and Americanism, there is a core

that I think is good. And there's a core that has formed so much of me that it's difficult for me to separate myself from it. It's difficult for me to separate myself as a human being from my Catholic upbringing, or from being an American. And in a minor way, it also reflects the way I feel about the Marvel Universe or the DC Universe. I love the DC Universe. I grew up with those characters. But you could argue that the DC Universe began with *Detective Comics* no. 1, which is rife with these really intense yellow-peril figures. So the foundation of these stories that I love, that I grew up with and that formed my conscience and my consciousness—they're rooted in something that's very anti-me.

BLVR: That's a really well-articulated conflict. Not to get too cheesy, but you said there's something at the core of America that's good. And there's something at the core of Catholicism that's good. I imagine those two things may be different. But what is "the good" for you?

GLY: For Catholicism, it's this idea that you are your truest self by participating in self-donating love. And for America… this is also very cheesy…

BLVR: It's great. I love it.

GLY: For America… OK, obviously, there are untold buckets of blood in American history. But the core idea is that a group of people can be bound by a set of ideals rather than by blood and soil. I think that's a really beautiful idea.

BLVR: Do you think we're making progress? On the Asian American stories front, Asian American comics are becoming TV shows and films, and Asian American films are winning Oscars. How authentically does that feel like progress to you?

GLY: I think it's K-shaped. I think we're both making progress and falling behind. The stories we tell do influence our culture and the way we think about each other. So the fact that there are Asian American stories on the streamers does reflect an acceptance of us as a community. But then you read about the violence that's perpetuated against us, and especially our elders, and that feels like a falling backward. And the division between different communities in America feels more stark than it used to.

BLVR: It's hard to know how to connect those upper and lower legs of the K.

GLY: To your point about Oscar winners, in *American Born Chinese*, Ke Huy Quan plays the character that stands in for cousin Chin-Kee, and we cast him very intentionally. Ke was Short Round in *Indiana Jones*. He was Data in *Goonies*. And then he had a couple of decades in the wilderness, where he would get offered these really terrible, stereotypical Asian roles, and eventually he left Hollywood because of that. Then he comes back and wins an Oscar. I think that really does show the upper part of that K.

BLVR: People are eager to tell the story of how we used to be racist and now we're not.

GLY: I think that's all of us. All of us want to tell that story. ✶

MICROINTERVIEW WITH NOOR NAGA, PART IV

THE BELIEVER: Questions about both arrogance and humility recur in *If an Egyptian Cannot Speak English*, and I was curious about what interests you about these themes, specifically.

NOOR NAGA: It's a deeply religious question, actually. The way a lot of faiths understand primal sin, especially in Islam, is that the root of all sin is arrogance—arrogance about God, thinking you are not a dependent being, not dependent on the divine. There's this idea of covering up what you know to be true. As someone who's a practicing Muslim, and who's deeply spiritual, I find this is the balance I'm constantly thinking about in my own life: arrogance versus humility. Because also you need a little bit of arrogance, which is sort of pride. It's not helpful to tip too much in the other direction. Humility can turn into a kind of self-hatred or self-erasure, or a smallness that is also not healthy. I'm interested in ego, what it means to keep your actual size as a person. Not getting too big and squashing people or things around you. But also not shrinking yourself so you're this little mouse of a person. Being human-sized. ✶

LASAGNA NATION
THE LIFE AND AFTERLIVES OF GARFIELD

by Anika Banister

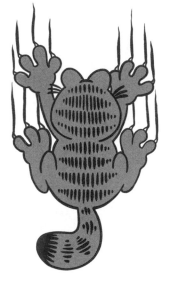

Seven years into his apprenticeship on the comic strip *Tumbleweeds*, adman turned cartoonist Jim Davis still wasn't close to his dream of syndication. By 1976, he had learned how to ink backgrounds and time a gag, but his own strip, *Gnorm Gnat*, hadn't gone any further than a local Indiana paper. His nonhuman protagonist was meant to ward off the controversy that *Tumbleweeds*' cowboys-and-Indians premise raked in, but as one editor told him: "Bugs? Nobody can relate."

Davis pulled his comic about the smarmy, squinty-eyed gnat that year, and filled the slot with a new strip called *Jon*. According to one of his colleagues, Davis's goals were modest: "All he really wanted was enough money to buy beer and cigarettes." Loosely based on his own life, it starred cartoonist Jon Arbuckle and his hulking, jowly beast of a cat, who assumed Gnorm's bad attitude and dour squint. Although the cat was only marginally easier on the eyes, he instantly became the star of the strip. Yet again, Davis's strip left the pages, only to return with a new name the next year. In 1978, *Garfield* debuted nationally in forty-one publications, and at thirty-two years old, Davis was finally on track to creating one of the biggest comic strips of all time.

In *Garfield*'s first year, *The Chicago Sun-Times* tried to pull the comic—but was met with over a thousand protesting phone calls and hundreds of letters. *Garfield*'s market domination matched the cat's personality. In a gag from the first month, Jon dangles a sausage, taunting, "Here, Garfield… Beg." Garfield swipes at his leg and snatches the meat, chewing pensively as he thinks, "Groveling is not one of my strong suits."

In 1981, Davis launched PAWS Inc., to handle the licensing of *Garfield* merchandise: the rights belonged to his syndicate, then called United Feature Syndicate, but Davis had creative control. Most cartoonists leave the merchandising to the syndicate and focus on the strip, but Davis had licensing in mind from the beginning. At the PAWS headquarters in Muncie, Indiana—the town that inspired the seminal study of Midwestern American culture, *Middletown*, a true American nowhere—he hired writers, artists, and other professionals to free him up to focus on the *Garfield* brand at large. Not that he took it easy: Davis worked sixty-hour weeks, with about a quarter of his time reserved for the strip itself.

The atmosphere at the Muncie compound resembled a modern-day tech start-up more than the home of a sleepy cartoon cat: employees clocking long hours, a product with meteoric success, and a visionary clutching the reins. "After our work during the day, Jim would buy us pizza, about five o'clock in the evening," recalled Gary Barker, a longtime artist for the strip, of the PAWS culture in 1983. "We would work until way late, as long as we needed." He kept a sleeping bag behind his desk.

Those hours yielded results. *Garfield*'s popularity skyrocketed in the '80s. The fat cat starred in Emmy-winning prime-time TV specials, and collections of the strips in a never-before-seen horizontal format (pioneered by Davis) came out every year. One week in 1982, seven of the ten slots on *The New York Times*' paperback bestseller list were *Garfield* titles, a feat that made publishing history. The same year, Garf even graced the cover of *People*, crowding out news about Christie Brinkley and the Eagles. In 1983, a Garfield balloon debuted at the Macy's Thanksgiving Day Parade, the biggest parade balloon ever by volume, according to Davis.

The strip matured along with the business. Peripheral figures, like Jon's roommate Lyman, and wacky

Illustrations throughout by the author

environments were less common, but the gags and character dynamics were still fresh. A gag might begin in the land of giant breakfasts, but Garfield always woke up in his familiar cat bed. Heavy merchandising fueled both the firm and its fandom. In 1987, PAWS introduced suction-pawed Garfield plushies for car windows. After selling 225 million in two years, PAWS pulled them from shelves, as they had become so popular that people were starting to break into cars to steal the plushies—*only* the plushies. But theft was a secondary concern: Davis stated that his biggest fear was overexposure.

The next year, *Garfield and Friends* began airing on Saturday mornings on CBS. Garfield's design had become sleeker to meet the technical challenges of his earlier animated specials, physical changes that seeped back into the strip. After there was some trouble animating Garfield's walk for the *Here Comes Garfield* special (1982), no less an expert than *Peanuts* creator Charles Schulz stepped in and drew Garfield with human-sized feet. Davis took the tip to heart: by the end of the decade, Garfield was a full-time bipedal in the strip, and a much slimmer one at that.

Garfield was now an economic force. Davis employed around fifty full-timers in Muncie, and personally earned about thirty million dollars a year, enough for all the beer and cigarettes he could want.

Davis was preoccupied by more than just paw size, however. He knew the world (and thus the market) was changing, and was determined to adapt. In the mid-'80s, everyone on staff was given a computer and ordered to learn how to "do email." In the early '90s, PAWS adopted the very first version of Photoshop. And in 1994, Davis made comics history with an unprecedented move: for somewhere between fifteen and twenty million dollars, he bought back the rights to his own comic strip. As the new millennium neared, Davis sensed that changes would come to the medium. In 1998, he predicted that in a decade or two, "the newspaper as we know it is going to evolve into something in the electronic environment. Young people are more comfortable staring at a computer screen or video monitor than they are at a piece of newsprint. That's the reality of the day."

Garfield was already well-suited for the internet: it was relatable on the most basic level (this cat loves food and hates work!), visually iconic, and culturally nonspecific. Nonspecific in all ways, really: when Davis's comment about Garfield having no race, nationality, or gender in a 2014 *Mental Floss* interview was dug up in 2017, a fierce Wikipedia war was waged over the cat's official gender. Someone with a congressional IP address weighed in.[1] *Garfield*, with its predictable timing, broad audience, and vast archives, was fertile material to be reimagined without having to keep the market in mind. In 1996, the strip went online, and fans, tired of the usual gags and armed with newfangled photo-editing software, started remixing.

Recontextualized comics were a phenomenon that had existed even before the internet—in zines, where elements of comics that people were bored with were swapped out for fans' (or haters') own material. *The Dysfunctional Family Circus* was a fan creation that gave Bil Keane's deeply trad midcentury comic, *The Family Circus*, new and foul captions. David Malki, creator of the webcomic *Wondermark*, discussed the phenomenon in a 2006 blog post: the paradox, he wrote, is that the more well known the original product is, "the riper a fruit it is for subversion." By the early aughts, nothing on the comics page was riper than *Garfield*. In 2002, it had entered the *Guinness World Records* as the most syndicated comic strip ever. At its peak, in 2004, the comic reached 2,600 daily papers and 260 million readers—if the math checks out, about 4 percent of the world's population. Yearly profits were somewhere in the ballpark of a billion dollars, easily clearing the total GDP of several small countries. But while the strip kept growing, many complained that its glory days were long over.

Enter the Garfield Randomizer, a script that pulled three random panels from the depths of the online *Garfield* archives and threw them into a single strip. It was funny when it didn't make sense, but even funnier when it did: Jon smugly saying, "Cheer up, Garfield"; Garfield raising a paw in defiance; Garfield slapping Jon in circles. The *Garfield* formula was so exacting and narrow that the Randomizer produced plausible results while bringing back the surreal edge found in the earlier comics. Davis has been open about keeping the backgrounds nondescript (despite a whiff of the American

---

1. It wasn't Garfield's first time in Congress: in 2003, Mike Pence wished happy birthday on the House floor to his state's most famous feline.

Midwest) so that readers around the world can relate, and about perfecting the strip's rhythm. Malki noted: "The unanimous sentiment online was that for the first time in years, *Garfield* was funny again."

Alas, within months, PAWS issued a cease and desist order, and the Randomizer project was shuttered—although the creator posted the code, which may be how copycat sites exist to this day. The most surprising element of this corporate backlash is that it seems to be the first and last time that PAWS cracked down on internet fandom. Malki addressed the corporate owner directly in a post: "Learn to recognize a compliment. We like your stuff. It has meaning to us, both as individuals and as a culture. We grew up with your characters, and so they have an emotional resonance for us that overflows with potential. Let them come out and play with us."

They did. *Garfield* variants proliferated in peace: *Realfield* (Garfield replaced by a real cat); *Garkov* (*Garfield* strips generated by text-predicting Markov chains fed by the archive); *Barfield* (don't ask). By 2008, PAWS was singing a different tune. When Davis and Ballantine, the publisher of all PAWS books, got wind of a *Garfield* variant that was taking off, they turned the content into an official *Garfield* book, with commentary from Davis and Dan Walsh, the variant's creator.

This was, of course, *Garfield Minus Garfield*, the best-known *Garfield* remix to date. Walsh simply erased Garfield from the strip, exposing Jon as a depressed guy in the suburbs talking to himself. It was a hit on campus; perhaps the 2008 financial crisis made this

1976
ELDRITCH HORROR
Proto-Garf debuts in the comic, Jon.

1978
MONGREL
Garfield *debuts.* The Chicago Sun-Times *tries to pull* Garfield, *is met with mass protest.*

1981
FINALLY FELINE
Jim Davis incorporates Garf, forming PAWS Inc.

1982
HOLLYWOOD DEBUTANTE
Garfield's feet swell in Here Comes Garfield, *the first of four Emmy-winning TV specials.*

1987
THE GOLDEN GARF
Garfield & Friends *airs; popular* Garfield *plushie drives the public to crime.*

1994
FAT-CAT'S FAT CAT
Jim Davis buys back PAWS Inc. for $15–$20 million.

kind of misery resonate with young millennials.

These early variants, and the leniency about intellectual property, laid the groundwork for today's flourishing *Garfield* meme culture. After the Garfield Randomizer came *Lasagna Cat*, a 2007 YouTube series staging absurdly high-quality live-action *Garfield* gags; *Garfielf* (2013), a deliberately low-quality animation of *Garfield*; and *ImsorryJon*, the absurd/creepy punch line for a swath of horror-themed memes in the late 2010s that started with a 2013 comic in which Garfield eats the house with Jon inside. After *ImsorryJon* came… *Lasagna Cat*, again? After a decade's hiatus,

it returned with a bang: a one-shot monologue about the brilliance of the surreal 1978 strip in which Garfield puffs on Jon's stolen pipe, set to Philip Glass's score to the film *Kundun*.

There have been countless viral *Garfield* memes over the last two decades, each trying to outdo its predecessor's absurdity. Straightforward derision in the aughts yielded to ironic fandom in the 2010s, which has turned into sincere stanning, flaws and all. The *Garfield* meme page @garfigment was created in June 2022 and quickly amassed eleven thousand followers, of whom about 60 percent are aged eighteen to twenty-four. (Some fan accounts, like @everydaygarfield, have hundreds of thousands of followers; more niche, chattier ones hover in the tens of thousands.) Vincent, the twenty-five-year-old account owner, described their fan base: "A large portion of the fans really are nostalgic for the old comics. [They like] how you can just have fun with them and make them into what you want." Vincent described a strip from the '70s that includes the lines "My uncle Barney went to the vet once. He came back as my aunt Bernice." Someone had dug up the strip and tacked on another panel with some new Garf commentary: "Trans fucking rights babey."

The early permissiveness that PAWS showed to online creators allowed a deluge of *Garfield* fan content to populate the internet, which is now constantly being rediscovered and remixed yet again in the era of stan accounts and social media archiving. It's easier than ever for young people to be exposed to *Garfield*, through memes or vintage merch, which has taken on a charming or cursed quality, depending on the item. (Lava lamp? Fuzzy

toilet seat cover?) *Garfield* remixing continues offline, too, thanks to the artists who turn out their own takes on *Garfield* in the form of fan comics, art zines, and even tattoo designs. Tiny Splendor, a small publishing collective in California, put out a 2021 fanzine of "Garfield-induced" content called *Garfield & Friends*, home to the smutty comics, alternate Garf-verses, and melancholy pandemic musings of sixty-four artists. According to Sanaa Khan, who spearheaded the project, everyone she contacted "turned out to be a secret *Garfield* fan." It features Louise Leong's guide to drawing our hero (with expressions ranging from "wonky" to "so fucking bored"), Robin Milliken's geometric abstraction "Rare Checkered Floors," and a spare, introspective riff by Jaakko Pallasvuo: "You didn't want to be Garfield anymore… you wanted to write poetry." Themes include Garfield going through a breakup; Garfield breaking up with you; drugs; femme and/or goth Garf-sonas; superhero Garf; depression; full-frontal Garf;

rim jobs; and the hundreds of Garf phones that have been washing up on a French beach for three decades— a mystery finally solved by the 2019 discovery of a hidden shipwreck.

Other artist-fans I spoke to consistently cited the weirder, less popular *Garfield* media as inspiration, like the book *Garfield: His 9 Lives*, a 1984 collection that experiments with different art styles and darker themes—much darker themes. The book is off-brand enough that it earned a 2011 *Family Guy* shout-out, in which Peter Griffin asks: "Why did you do *Garfield: His 9 Lives*, Jim Davis? Why did you do that dark, freaky one where Garfield kills that old woman?" (One of the vignettes in the book suggests that Garfield's hatred of the vet stems from his past life as a tortured lab cat.) Amy Beardemphl, a graphic designer in Seattle, is a fan; in her free time, she draws Sad Cat, starring a burping, alcoholic Garf, reimagined as a depressed former child star bickering with TV's Alf at the bar. These "copyright infringement comics" have been published in underground zines

2004	2006	2008	2019

TABBY AT THE TOP	**MEME REBIRTH**	**INDIE GARF**	**LEGEND LET LOOSE**
Garfield's circulation peaks at 260 million, breaking records; Bill Murray mistakes screenwriter Cohen for Coen brother, decides to star in Garfield, the Movie.	*Fans reject the modern, soullessly sleek Garfield and create DIY gag images; the Garfield Randomizer is promptly served a cease and desist.*	*Garfield Minus Garfield receives universal mainstream praise; Publishers Weekly says: "If Samuel Beckett had been a strip cartoonist, he might've produced something like this."*	*Jim Davis retires, sells Garfield to a global conglomerate; a French beach town solves a decades-old mystery of Garfield phones washing ashore.*

in Seattle, New York, and Quebec. Even though *Garfield* was built to reach the widest-possible audience, the smaller successes seem to have secured a cult legacy of their own.

Few media empires are able to attract mainstream and indie fandom. Naomi Fry, a lifelong fan and *New Yorker* staff writer, believes that creatives are drawn to Garfield's passive defiance, which she describes as "the attitude of a critic," and integral to her childhood. "Garfield is ultimately a cynical commentator with some remnant of hope within him," she mused, "and if you're talking about creative people, or people who are still trying to do something in the world, you want to believe that what you're saying matters, while at the same time knowing it probably doesn't really matter. It's also a kind of deniability! You don't want to come out stupid. I think a lot of people are careful about putting themselves out on the line, because there are so many ways in which you can be humiliated, especially now, when everything is public."

The official *Garfield* brand continues to expand in the twenty-first century, but the newer media doesn't receive the same kind of love. The 2000s movies *Garfield: A Tail of Two Kitties* and *Garfield: The Movie* raked in cash and critical lashings alike; the many mobile *Garfield* games surpassed thirty million downloads in 2014, with negligible cultural impact. And after a career fighting for control of his strip, Davis is loosening the reins in his mid-seventies: in 2019, he sold the *Garfield* property to what is now Paramount Global (Nickelodeon's parent) for an undisclosed sum. The company immediately announced a new video game series, a TV show, and a movie. (Online, fans are already bemoaning the upcoming 2024 *Garfield* movie, bewildered by Chris Pratt's role as Garfield.) The only part Davis held on to was the strip itself, "the thing that gets me out of bed every morning."

In a series of 1989 Halloween strips, Garfield wakes up in an alternate dimension: dark, askew, and uninhabited. He's cursed to live on without his caretaker in a universe unlike anything he's ever known, and he finds it unbearable, retreating to his imagination to reunite with Jon and Odie—and so the strip continues as normal. The omniscient narrator (unique in the canon) intones: "After years of taking life for granted, Garfield is shaken by a horrifying vision of the inevitable process called 'time.'" Outside the strip, Garfield faces a similarly ravaged landscape today, as newspapers slash their funny pages to compete with the internet. But due in part to Davis's market clairvoyance, time has been kinder to the gluttonous feline himself, who may end up being the last great face of the funnies. Davis may be winding down, but his creation seems to have found the secret of eternal life, thanks to media monoliths and online fanatics alike. Garfield's fate brings to mind the last line from "Space Cat," the ninth of *His 9 Lives*: "I'm a hero, and heroes don't die." ✶

ALL PORTALS AND THEIR DESTINATIONS IN MOHSIN HAMID'S *EXIT WEST*

✶ Surry Hills, Sydney ←→ unspecified location

✶ Shinjuku, Tokyo ←→ Philippines

✶ La Jolla, San Diego ←→ unspecified location

✶ Neighborhood not far from Nadia's (in Saeed and Nadia's city) ←→ unspecified location

✶ Unspecified location ←→ Jumeirah Beach Residence, Dubai, UAE

✶ Saeed and Nadia's city ←→ Mykonos, Greece

✶ Saeed and Nadia's country ←→ Vienna

✶ Mykonos, Greece ←→ Germany

✶ Mykonos, Greece ←→ London

✶ London ←→ Nigeria

✶ London ←→ Somalia

✶ London ←→ borderlands between Myanmar and Thailand

✶ Kentish Town, London ←→ Namibia

✶ Hills above Tijuana, Mexico ←→ unspecified location

✶ Prinsengracht, Amsterdam ←→ Santa Teresa, Brazil

✶ A place nearby London ←→ Marin County, California, United States

✶ In the hills outside Marrakech, Morocco ←→ unspecified location

—list compiled by Gabe Boyd

JEFF DANIELS

[ACTOR, MUSICIAN, WRITER]

"IF YOU PLAY YOUR AGE, THAT'S THE BEST YOU'LL EVER BE."

Products advertised by Jeff Daniels in the '70s and '80s:
Pepto Bismol
Sure deodorant
Ore-Ida Tater Tots
Head & Shoulders shampoo

Jeff Daniels began performing, somewhat reluctantly, as a sophomore in high school in the '70s and has not stopped since. Over the past five decades, he's appeared in fifty-seven films, fourteen television series, seven Broadway productions, and numerous off-Broadway shows. His prolific creative output extends beyond acting too: he's written over a dozen plays and hundreds of songs; directed and produced; and toured the country as a singer-songwriter. And he has done all this from an unlikely location. Except for a few years in New York City immediately after he dropped out of Central Michigan University, Daniels has always lived in the same small town where he grew up: Chelsea, Michigan.

Daniels's father was at various times the mayor of Chelsea and its school board president. He was also the second-generation owner of a local lumberyard, which is now co-owned by Jeff's brother. Daniels was often cast in on-screen roles that were wholesome or a little naive, reflecting his small-town background: in 1998's

Illustration by Kristian Hammerstad

Pleasantville, *as a 1950s soda fountain operator; in 1985's* The Purple Rose of Cairo, *as a wide-eyed film star within a film who leaps off the screen and into Mia Farrow's real life; in 1986's* Something Wild, *as an unwitting accomplice to Melanie Griffith's illicit adventures. Of that Midwestern-ness, Daniels says that at first it was "either something to overcome or something to defend. And then it was something to be and not apologize for. So I didn't change who I was, whatever that looked like to casting directors. I'm also not pretty. Handsome. I wasn't that, and I knew I wasn't that."*

He took a wild left turn into mainstream comedy as Jim Carrey's sidekick in 1994's Dumb and Dumber, *which ultimately cultivated what Daniels calls a "creative fearlessness." It's hard to find a genre in which Daniels has not dabbled, whether as leading man or in a supporting role. He's in romantic comedies and gritty, hard-bitten contemporary streaming series. He's in an outer space movie, an apocalypse movie, a western, several based-on-a-true-story dramas. Daniels has played George Washington, FBI agent John O'Neill, and Apple executive John Sculley. At least four times he's appeared on-screen as a troubled novelist or frustrated writer. He brings a gravitas to many of his roles, as he did with his Tony-nominated year-plus run on Broadway as Atticus Finch. But he's never stopped being funny, and even tender, especially in indie films like* The Squid and the Whale *and* Away We Go. *And, largely to keep himself from being bored, he's never stopped trying new things. This fall he'll appear in season two of* American Rust, *a new adaptation of* A Man in Full, *as well as in an Audible Original podcast,* Alive and Well Enough.

In 1991, when Daniels returned to Chelsea from New York, he founded the nonprofit Purple Rose Theatre Company, which produces world-class original and classic plays with Actors' Equity Association casts. Daniels is the artistic director. The day he and I met in Chelsea, he planned to go into the theater after we spoke. "The theater coming back from the pandemic was hard. We had to win 'em back," he told me. Last fall, they had a hit play—that he wrote—about pickleball. I asked him why he thought a comedy about pickleball was such a success. "Well, the pulse of the culture is: Make me laugh! *That's what we heard in the fall of 2022, coming out of COVID:* I need to laugh. Just make me laugh about something. Anything."

I live a few towns over from Chelsea, and he and I had met before. For this conversation—which took place before the SAG-AFTRA strike began—Daniels invited me to a big barn that he and his sons had converted into a recording studio. It's used for his sons' musical endeavors, and also for Daniels's singer-songwriter work, audiobook recordings, and quick audio fixes that used to require him to fly to New York just to repair a line or two of dialogue. It's also, apparently, a site for golf practice. A huge black net and a set of clubs occupy one wall of the live room. The entire building is worn-in and mellow in the right ways, with several shapeless couches, a snack-stocked kitchen, and a cozy upstairs writing room filled with CDs, books, framed concert posters, and at least fifty guitars installed on a rack, retail-showcase-style. We talked in the writing room, which was quiet except for the birds trilling in a tree outside.

—Amanda Uhle

I. "MOVING FOR US IS CREATING"

THE BELIEVER: I was going to ask about your guitar—singular—but you have a collection.

JEFF DANIELS: It's more of an accumulation than a collection. There are about twelve Martin guitars, and there's one from 1924, one from 1937. I got a whole list of them, and the serial numbers and the whole deal. I don't go to guitar stores anymore, just because I don't need all that. But they're like pieces of art. Most of them appreciate in value if you take care of them. I got the guitar that I had in *The Newsroom*. And *American Rust*, the show set around Pittsburgh.

BLVR: What does having a guitar in your hands do for you that acting doesn't?

JD: You know, I was talking to Jim Carrey. We were on one of the promotional tours for *Dumb and Dumber To*, and we were flying back, and I just said, "I don't know. I think I'm done. I just don't—I don't know." He goes, "You? No, you can't quit." He said, "We're like sharks. We have to keep moving, and moving for us is creating. We're wired that way." And it's annoying because it doesn't ever turn off. But when you're an actor and you're sitting there waiting for the phone to ring, that's what drives you nuts. You rely on other people to decide that you're good enough to work. And that's why the writing thing started to happen. And the music was always something I just wanted—to learn how to play acoustic guitar. I'd started out in high school musicals, right? So I really liked Arlo Guthrie and Steve Goodman and James Taylor and John Prine in the '70s. People like Utah Phillips. Songwriting on the guitar was something I could always do to keep creatively sane. Especially early in New York, I'm sitting in one room on Twenty-Third and Seventh for two years. And I'm twenty-one. Don't know anybody. I have Circle Rep [the Circle Repertory Company, where Daniels began as an apprentice in 1976], but I just… You're a babe in the woods. And that guitar was my best friend.

BLVR: Waiting like that is demoralizing.

JD: I waited and waited. And so you just call your agent. You call on a Tuesday, "Hey, just, you know, checking in, checking in." [*Laughs*] "Just letting you know that I'm here, you know. Anything… anything going on? Commercials, TV, anything? Any plays? No? Nothing?" And then your agent says, "Nope. Have a good weekend."

BLVR: On a Tuesday?

JD: A Tuesday. So the guitar became a place to write. A thing that just kept me sane. And then around 2000, the acting career started to slow down, as they tend to do. When you get older, suddenly it's "Get me a younger Jeff Daniels." The opportunities dry up. The money gets lower. It just feels like it's over. And so what are you gonna do now? You're in your early fifties. Yeah, you had a great little run with *Dumb and Dumber* and *Gettysburg*. But that's not gonna happen anymore. So I just picked up the guitar.

I looked back into the songs I'd been working on for thirty years, and I pulled out ones that could work if I were to walk onto a stage in front of two hundred people at the Ark [in Ann Arbor, Michigan] or somewhere on the folk circuit. I could be happy doing that. So I did. I've played for the last twenty-five years—over five hundred gigs. Even if it was fifty people—I just thought the money would be less; we'd have to get rid of some things and change the way we live—I could be creatively happy doing that.

BLVR: Engaging your mind.

JD: And then I got *The Newsroom*. And now suddenly you're back in business.

BLVR: Very few actors get to do that, once they feel they're done.

JD: Well, it's not that you're done. It's that they just don't want you anymore. Or want you in the same way. They're done with you. That's what the guitar did and the writing does—I'm the only one who decides when I'm done on those two things.

II. THAT EVERYDAY LOOK

BLVR: I have done my YouTube homework [*laughs*] on some of your early commercials that you did in the late '70s. First of all, you took a completely shameless approach to taking jobs for any kind of embarrassing product. There's the deodorant, there's Tater Tots.

JD: Tater Tots. Oh god.

BLVR: You play a college student with diarrhea in a Pepto Bismol one. And you're amazing. You exude joy in this commercial. And you exude a little bit of your Midwesternness, whether you wanted to or not, but it's beautiful. How did you feel? Did you feel the joy that you were exuding or were you feeling, like, Thank god I got a job?

JD: [*Laughs*] I'd had a lot of acting classes by that point, and learned how to inhabit characters. You learn how to think like that character. Yeah, in that commercial we were five hundred college kids who had diarrhea. And I'm there telling my parents on parents' weekend about how some of us took Pepto Bismol—and, boy, did it work! And then the father mutters, "He passes one test in college, and it was a diarrhea test." That was a funny commercial.

BLVR: You just delivered that verbatim.

JD: I can almost remember the actor. He was a New York actor. I don't remember his name. Grumpy old guy with a Hawaiian shirt and

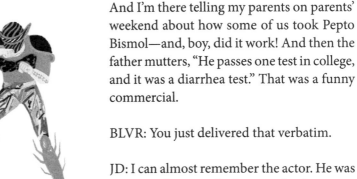

a camera on a strap in front of him. Probably did the scene sixty times. You know, with commercials, they overshoot the shit out of them.

BLVR: You felt good doing those commercials?

JD: Well, yes. I did an off-Broadway play as soon as I got to New York in 1976, and it got panned by the critics. I didn't know what I was doing. I completely froze up. But an agent came down to see the guy who played my father, a guy named Jack Gwillim, a sixty-five-year-old English actor who was great in the play. I was his son who was feckless. So Jack's agent came down, a guy named Milton Goldman at ICM, and he asked, "Who's the kid?" So now I'm going to see an agent. And Milton couldn't have been nicer, but one of the things he said was "We're gonna send you down to the commercial department, see if you can

---

MICROINTERVIEW WITH NOOR NAGA, PART V

THE BELIEVER: Do you think a good writer is suspicious of themselves? How much self-criticism do you allow into your writing practice?

NOOR NAGA: I think my writing practice is entirely self-criticism and suspicion. It's a vaguely masochistic impulse, but I don't think that's necessary, or the only way. I think that's just my way. I'm like a scab picker. I just want to look at things that are uncomfortable. I want to live in the uncomfortable place. And I want to invite readers into that uncomfortable place. I think there's a lot of learning that happens there.

BLVR: How can someone become a better reader?

NN: That's a very strange question. It's like saying, *How can someone be a better walker or sitter?* I don't know that there is a better or a worse way to read. I think people bring their own worlds to what they're reading, and I'm very OK with that. ✶

make us some money. You got a look—that Midwestern look, that everyday look, not the movie star look." And, you know, bang. I started getting commercials.

BLVR: Dandruff shampoo. Tater Tots.

JD: All of which meant I didn't have to wait tables. I didn't have to drive a cab in '70s New York.

BLVR: Did you ever drive a cab?

JD: No, because I was doing commercials. You go on twenty auditions to get one. Make that forty. That's how you make rent. They pay you every time it's on, in thirteen-week cycles. Ten grand for a national commercial over three months was a lot of money in New York in the '70s.

III. THE MAN WITH ONE ARM

BLVR: Some writers, as their careers go on, feel like their minds are being sharpened. But actors use their bodies, and the body deteriorates with age. I watched the first episode of *Godless* this week, and I saw you riding a horse with one hand behind your back, at whatever age you were when that show came out. I couldn't do that, at any age. How do you ride a horse with one arm? And how do you use your body better and better as your career goes on?

JD: I think about guys like Jack Lemmon and [Robert] De Niro, who didn't get the plastic surgery, who said, *This is how old I am now. This is what I look like.* And you play those roles. You don't try to play ten years or fifteen years younger. First of all, we all already know how old you are. We can just google you.

BLVR: It's on the internet.

JD: You're not fooling anybody. I understand wanting to look good and not wanting to deteriorate. But, you know, Jimmy Stewart was Jimmy Stewart older. Laurence Olivier was older. This is what I look like. And so you play roles of that age. The great thing is that you are now an encyclopedia of acting—not only in front of the camera, but on set. You know how to pace yourself, how to stay ready on one and two. And an [Aaron] Sorkin speech doesn't take you ten takes to figure out what you're doing. If you play your age, that's the best you'll ever be. You know so much—far more than you did thirty years ago, when you were in such and such a movie. That was just instinct. That was just talent.

BLVR: How do you prepare for a role now?

JD: We were doing *The Newsroom*, the second season, and Jane Fonda emailed me. She was gonna play my boss, Leona Lansing. She said, "Tell me what to do. I hear it's *Don't change a word, and it's so fast.*" I mean, she was going, "Help me out here. How do I do this?" I said, "At six in the morning, when you get there, you have to know it and know what you're gonna do with it on take one."

BLVR: You're not turning to anybody else in those situations.

JD: Execute what was intended when they wrote it. You have to prepare. You have to memorize it and memorize it and memorize it and rep it and rep it like an athlete on a football field. In training camp, they're throwing the same screen pass every single day. The guitar players are doing the same riff. They practice over and over and over. So now you're not even thinking about that big Northwestern [University] speech that you gave [in *The Newsroom*]. You know, it's two pages long, full of numbers and switches, and you can roll it while you're washing dishes. You can roll it while you're going to Whole Foods. The words roll one after another after another. Then you gotta be able to pick up the pace in *The Newsroom*'s case, so you're able to roll it at Sorkin's pace.

Now when they say, "Action," it happens for the first time. And now you're using the other actor, which is where half your performance is. And we're not taught that. What we're taught is: *I'm ready for my close-up, Mr. DeMille. Me, me, me, me, me, me, me.*

BLVR: You're putting so much trust in another person.

JD: It's true, unless you're doing a monologue. There's someone else in the scene. And there's conflict because it's drama. Drama is conflict. Every scene has to have that. You're going back and forth. And it's tennis, verbal tennis. How

does she say that? The way she said it, do I lean in to hear it or react? [*Winces*] Use what she's given you to hit it back.

IV. WHERE IS FUNNY?

JD: You have to know where funny is.

BLVR: How did you learn that?

JD: I found it going onstage in a high school musical. The sixth-grade music teacher ended up being the high school choir director—it's a very small town. She would later pluck guys out of the chorus: "You, I need you in *South Pacific*." But in sixth grade, she said, "We're not gonna do any music today. Let's just do skits. I've made up some things you can act out." And it was improv. A couple kids did stuff. And then: "Jeff, OK, you're a politician who's giving a speech and your pants are falling down." So I went up and said whatever a sixth grader says about today's issues, thank you very much. I'm winging it on what a mayor would do, and then I started with a little tug at the belt and then just grabbing one side and continuing to talk, and then grabbing with both hands [*grabs his pants, makes various horrified facial expressions*]. And by the end of it, my pants looked like they weighed two hundred pounds. And I was trying to hold them up while still talking about how the community needs a road. [*Laughs*]

I didn't rehearse it. She went to my parents and she said, "Keep an eye on this one." Then later, in high school, I'm walking by after a bad basketball practice and she was waiting for me. She was doing auditions for *South Pacific* and she needed guys for the sailors. "Jeff!" Oh god, I thought. [*Laughs*] "Come here. I want you to audition for this." You couldn't say no to her. I got up there and they started doing "There Is Nothin' Like a Dame." All I had to do was dance, you know? So I got up and just started doing this [*rises and does a poker-faced knees-up jig around his writing room*]. And I knew it looked stupid. I was a sophomore. But I never broke. Straight face. I only had two lines in the thing. Radio operator, Bob McCaffrey, two lines in *South Pacific*. But I did that dance. Seven hundred people from town are cracking up. You just—you know where funny is.

Not everybody knows. Well, my dad knew. My dad could tell a story. And everyone laughed. I remember being on the stairs and my parents had bridge club. Suddenly he's stopping bridge club. He's telling about a thing that happened at the lumber company, and it's a ten-minute story. And all twelve people are laughing at my dad. They're with him and he's standing up in the middle of the room, killing. I remember just being on the stairs watching that.

V. SUPER SUCKER

BLVR: On the subject of comedy, *Super Sucker* is one of the great funny movies of our time, and one of the great feminist movies.

JD: God, I wish I'd sat down and said, *I'm gonna write a feminist film*. But it is!

BLVR: It came out twenty years ago. Is there a Hollywood studio that would've done it—then or now—with that premise?

JD: Working with Jim Carrey on *Dumb and Dumber* taught me how to be fearless—I've been creatively fearless ever since then.

Christopher Guest, the great independent comedic filmmaker with his troupe of hysterical people in movie after movie—I wanted that. I thought I could take a shot at that. And the first, most obvious one out of the plays I'd written was *Escanaba in da Moonlight*, which is about five guys in a deer camp. So we raised enough money to do that. And then, you know, nobody bought it. And we four-walled it [self-funded and distributed it]. And it played, well, where people hunt, in the Midwest and stuff. But we never made any money on it.

But I wanted to take one more shot at it. So I needed to write a funny Midwestern something. And then I came across the vacuum cleaner salesmen. The oddball people that are making a go of it in the small towns of America and will do pretty much anything. I just thought it was funny or certainly could be ripe for the kinds of interactions that lead to a story. I used a lot of the same people that we used in *Escanaba*, and we shot it in Jackson [Michigan]. The idea was that we were in a vacuum-cleaner-salesman war. Me and a guy on the other side of town, played by Harve Presnell. We were in a duel, and whoever sold the

most vacuum cleaners in a month would still be in business. The other guy would be fired. Something like that. Simple.

My character, who was losing, came up with this thing called the Homemaker's Little Helper. It's a vacuum cleaner that becomes, you know, a sexual device to be used… when you're alone. [*Laughs*] And so that's what he sells.

I remember the night in Jackson when we were gonna shoot this big scene, with all the women who used Homemaker's Little Helper. I was gonna stand on top of a van and basically parody the speech that Mel Gibson gave in *Braveheart*, while holding up the Homemaker's Little Helper. [*Holds imaginary vacuum wand*] *This is freedom!* Word had gotten out about what the movie was about, and it wasn't well received in all parts of Jackson.

BLVR: But you needed extras.

JD: So we put the word out.

BLVR: How are you explaining this to the extras? Is it a little bit of a surprise?

JD: Yeah. We didn't really tell them what we were doing. We said, "It's just a great vacuum cleaner, and you think it's the best vacuum cleaner you've ever had in your lives." [*Laughs*] But by that point, by the time we shot that scene, everybody had kind of figured it out. Back then, radio would help you: *Hey, volunteers! Want to go on a big scene with Jeff Daniels running down Michigan Avenue? Come on out tonight at seven o'clock,* you know. *Bring your mops and we'll give you a sign. Homemakers and housewives. Hope you can be there.* We were hoping for two hundred people.

BLVR: How many came?

JD: Five thousand. [*Laughs*] Five thousand women.

BLVR: In Jackson?

JD: In Jackson. Five thousand women came out, and we ran down that street with Homemaker's Little Helpers. Yeah. It's a feminist film.

VI. SPIDERS

BLVR: I thought a spider had been named after you. I looked it up. It's not a spider. [*Consults notes*] It's a tarantula-killing parasitic worm.

JD: Yes. [*Smiles*]

BLVR: Did you have a hand in requesting that designation?

JD: They had some national conference around arachnids. People who love spiders have some national organization. And they decided to honor me by naming a new something they'd found that needed a name. And for those folks, you know, *Arachnophobia* is their *Citizen Kane*. So they thought, Who could we possibly name this spider—or this whatever-it-was—after? They said, "We'll get Jeff." My agent called and said, "You're not gonna believe this one." [*Laughs*] I was all for it.

BLVR: I think it's much funnier, and more of an honor, because this was thirty-some years after the film.

JD: Well, again, it is their *Citizen Kane*. Yeah.

VII. "THE WRITING HAS TO BE SO GOOD"

BLVR: You have a wild range. When I look at the roles you've played, they go from the head of NASA to the outlaw in a Western, the news anchor, the romantic lead. And the films and shows are really of different genres. You're in a Martian movie.

JD: *The Martian.* I was the only guy in the movie going, *Hey, first of all, you know, you could die. All right. I'm just saying, I know all seven of you want to get onboard and go to Mars. But I'm just, I'm gonna be the guy that says, "You're probably not coming back."* And then at the same time, we all read the script. [*Laughs*] I know you're gonna go get him. And the reason you're gonna get him is because he is Matt Damon. We're not gonna go to Mars and find out he's dead.

BLVR: We are in a Matt Damon movie…

JD: Right. He's coming back somehow.

BLVR: Do you ever think twice about a role that's offered up? Maybe because something's not to your taste? I'm sure you say no to plenty of things all the time, but looking at the million roles you've done, I can't tell what your taste actually is. What do you like?

JD: Oh my god. That's great.

BLVR: Do they know what to send you?

JD: I think it has to be good writing. The writing has to be so good. Because if it isn't, I'll get bored and I won't be challenged and I'll want off it. I know I will end up being that guy—where it isn't worth it to me anymore. I think with something like *The Newsroom*, you also are riding a wave where you scored in a way they hadn't thought you could. And now you're getting better roles—I mean, *Good enough for Aaron Sorkin.* Maybe you get Scott Frank. Danny Futterman and Adam Rapp doing *The Looming Tower* off Lawrence Wright's book.

BLVR: You just move with it.

JD: I think it's chasing good writing, because that is what has kept me interested as the streamers started happening. There's twenty of them now. Twenty-five of them. And they all need writers. The streaming companies are where the writers went when Hollywood started doing the tentpole movies. Those are all great—the action movies, Marvel movies—and that's what Hollywood now is, basically. I started doing a lot of independent movies that nobody saw, but I really liked the scripts. And I was doing some off-Broadway stuff. More quirky, a little more complex, maybe.

So that has been a focus, and has driven a lot of the decisions. *A Man in Full* [forthcoming on Netflix], the Tom Wolfe book. David E. Kelly is the writer on it. That's it. They want me? Let's do a Zoom meeting. Let's do it. And Regina King was directing. She won an Oscar. I mean, surrounding yourself with that caliber of people, even if you've never worked with them before, is important. They see something in you that they think you can blow up and become Charlie Croker [the main character in *A Man in Full*]? A lot of that has to do with making the choice to do a *Dumb and Dumber* and going way out there with Jim Carrey. So you create this wide kind of range. You've made it possible for people to go, "Let's try him. I think he might be able to do this." That's exciting. That was kind of my little plan. ★

With a record number of families opting to homeschool in the wake of the pandemic, an enduring American question has resurfaced: What, exactly, is school for?

by **LAUREN MARKHAM**

illustrations by **MADISON KETCHAM**

It was Friday evening, an hour before showtime, and the art deco theater in San Luis Obispo, California, already had a line of well-dressed women circling the block, bound for the Wild + Free conference. They'd come from far and wide for a special weekend—hundreds of homeschooling "mamas" gathering "for two days of insight, inspiration, encouragement, and community," as the website promised.

Pauline Cook had traveled all the way from Central Washington. Before she became a mother, she had not heard of homeschooling. Now, over a decade later, with two teens and a twelve-year-old, she's a pro. There are as many ways to homeschool as there are families doing it—and there are families joining homeschool folds every day—but Pauline refers to her particular flavor as "Gospel-powered life school." This was her third Wild + Free conference. She'd attended her first five years earlier in search of resources. But she'd been surprised to find that Wild + Free wasn't just a place to share ideas—it was really a convening rooted in shared *purpose*.

"For as long as humans have lived on this earth," Wild + Free's founder, Ainsley Arment, has written, "children have been schooled at home." Arment is a homeschooling mother of five, and the modest Instagram account she started on parenting has now grown into something of an empire, offering monthly homeschool bundles, books, talks, retreats at a Virginia farm camp (you can pay extra to ride a zip line), a blog, and the annual Wild + Free conference, held this year in San Luis Obispo. "We may not all homeschool the same," as the conference invitation put it, "but we're in this together."

Pauline was dedicated to homeschool because it allowed her to spend valuable time with her children— time she knew was temporary—and to foster a sense of joy, wonder, creativity, and, yes, devotion to Christ, that can be difficult to achieve within the rat race of conventional society and institutional school. But above all, she wanted to protect her children's childhood. As a new homeschool mom, she'd found Wild + Free on Instagram, and it became a lifeline for her. Certain posts ("Life is messy, chaotic and full of distractions, which means learning at home will be too. But it can still be rich and beautiful") meant to inspire confidence in homeschoolers like Pauline when it wobbles. Other posts ("Home is not better than school if it is not a haven for a child's heart, mind and body") were reminders of what was most important in the homeschooling journey, to strengthen one's resolve.

In San Luis Obispo, Pauline queued up with the others in the shadow of the marquee. Inside, the atmosphere was electric. The other mothers ("While we value the vital role of fathers in homeschooling… this event is for women only," the promotional materials read) were dressed for the occasion: long boho dresses, high-heeled boots, perfectly tailored jeans, bowler hats, and beachy waves. They greeted one another with cheer, snacked on canapés, and crowded the maker stalls, where other attendees sold handmade journals and jewelry and hawked company schwag.

This was the Wild + Free community—women engaged in a vocation that can be remarkably demanding, has no clear map, and can also be quite isolating—together in the flesh. Arment liked to remind people that in spite of the fact that throughout history most education has happened outside of institutional schools, "we homeschooling mamas often feel like pioneers forging a new path for the next generation."

Pauline was here to reconnect with others based on that shared purpose she'd encountered at earlier conferences—to, as she put it, "refill my cup." She took a seat inside the theater; soon, the lights dimmed, and the screen lit up with a five-minute countdown. Then a video appeared, and the hall of women fell into a hush.

The camera began at the doorway to a home, then opened into a slightly out-of-focus living room, emptied of people. "This old house," a woman's voice narrated over the picture, "these quiet halls, these empty rooms, whisper from the past." It was Ainsley Arment's voice. The video then moved through the house's tidy rooms: a bunk room with mussed sheets, a dining room, a piano with two toy trucks perched on its rim—all "evidence of a life once lived together," Arment said. The long dining room table was set only for two now, for "childhood slips away like the turn of autumn."

The video cut to a pair of hands slowly washing a spoon at the kitchen sink. "We long for it to stay like this forever," Arment's narration continued. "But children grow up; that's what they do." The woman on-screen brewed a cup of tea and looked longingly out the window. "Dear Mama, whatever wounds you're mending, this, too, shall pass. The hardship, the heartache, the hopeless nights are only a small part of your family's story."

But what brought tears to Pauline's eyes was what came next: "All the good, all the love, all the beauty and blessings—they, too, will pass much sooner than we'd like." Pauline's kids were growing up. "The days are long," the oft-quoted parenting adage goes, "but the years are short." Soon, Pauline understood, would come a season of endings, of transition, of her children moving on.

The screen brightened, the woman came into focus, and the music began to surge and lift. "But not today," Arment's voice rang through the crowded rows of women. "Today, Mama, is meant for you. Today, Mama, is meant for *them*." The on-screen mama turned, and in through the back door ran four smiling children who leaped into her arms.

Across the theater sat another woman, named Trisha. This was her first conference, and she was stunned to find herself—not five minutes into the official program—also already in tears. Unlike Pauline, Trisha was new to the whole homeschool enterprise. The early pandemic virtual learning just hadn't worked for her kids, as for so many children and families. In late 2020, she took what she'd thought would be a temporary leave from her job as a physical therapist in Texas to tend to her children's education—just until school reopened and things returned to normal. Except that she fell in love with it. Her kids never went back to school.

In Texas she'd joined a Wild + Free meetup group, where she connected with other homeschool parents and arranged regular outings with them and their kids. When she and her husband decided to move their family back to her hometown in Hawaii, she started a Wild + Free group of her own. Trisha was secular, but the references to faith that permeated Wild + Free didn't bother her. At the root, she felt, all the Wild + Free folks wanted the same thing: to live outside the frenzy of a bell schedule and standardized testing, to spend as much time with their kids as they could while they were young, to put their children first.

Recently, though, Trisha had been doubting herself. Her in-laws questioned her decision to homeschool, and while her husband supported it, he felt she should be offering a more standardized curriculum than the free-flowing, child-driven format she favored—hiking to a waterfall one day, cooking and reading together the next—and in which she felt her children thrived. She'd justified coming to the conference because she needed resources. But sitting in that auditorium, she understood why she'd really come: for recognition from this sea of other mothers like her, and for validation that she and her family were on the right path.

"You are needed," Arment's voice boomed through the auditorium as the woman on-screen embraced her children. "All of you: the parts that can bear it, and the parts that can't. The perfectly imperfect version of you. Because at the end of the day, you are exactly the mother your children need."

There were around eight hundred homeschooling mamas in the room that day. Some, like Pauline, were old hands. But many others, like Trisha, had turned to homeschool as a result of the pandemic and never looked back. Based on data from the twenty-one states that track homeschooling enrollment, the practice has risen by 30 percent nationally since 2020. The actual numbers are likely far higher, according to education researcher Thomas Dee. "Notably," he writes in a recent report for the Urban Institute, "this dramatic increase reflects enrollment during the *second* full school year under the pandemic, when most schools returned to in-person instruction." Even when it was possible to send kids back to school, parents like Trisha opted not to. Now roughly 6 percent of the country's school-aged children are opting out of school in favor of learning at home.

I was in that auditorium too. I'd come because, as a longtime school administrator who had recently left my job in the Oakland, California, public schools, I was interested in the mass defection from institutional school: what it signified and what it heralded. I was also a new mother—suddenly included in the "mama" class—and thus charged with making decisions for a small being that rendered questions of school choice and educational philosophy far more personal than they had been before.

The video ended, and a cheery homeschooling husband-and-wife folk band took the stage, entreating the crowd to "sing along, or whistle along," to their hits including "Love Makes a Family," "The Best Love," and "Glory Days," because "this time with our kids is the glory days." Toward the end of the evening, the lights dimmed once again, and Arment walked onto the stage. With a laugh, she apologized for making everyone cry. "The title of my talk tonight," she said, "is 'The Lost Children'"—referring to all the children who had lost their way in this world as a result of leaving their parents' nests too early and going to school.

"Together, we stand in the face of all that society tells us and proclaim what is right for our house," she said to the crowd. Both Pauline and Trisha felt bolstered by this. This wasn't just a room full of mothers now, but of activists, trailblazers, believers, *pioneers.*

"We are here together for such a time as this," Arment declared as her talk came to a close, which I took to mean a time of maternal reawakening to both the wonders of childhood and the potential perils of institutional school. "I believe we can change the world," she said to the auditorium through the trembling of tears. "I believe we already are."

ere's a list of reasons parents gave me for choosing to homeschool:

Because, like Pauline, they are guided by Christ and want to integrate the gospel into their lessons. Because, like Trisha believes, children shouldn't be at desks all day, and they learn best when their interests guide the curriculum rather than the other way around. Because schools are racist. Because schools require vaccinations. Because they are afraid their children will get COVID. Because schools are increasingly banning books. Because schools are teaching books that parents find inappropriate or offensive. Because of school shootings. Because schools teach stuff that is wildly irrelevant for the future in a world that is vastly remaking itself before our eyes. Because schools are failing, as evidenced by crap test scores and national teacher shortages. Because schools aren't challenging students enough. Because of bullying. Because schools have a "trans agenda." Because schools are pawns of the educational-industrial complex. Because schools are pawns of the woke agenda. Because schools are hostile to trans children. Because schools don't serve neurodiverse children well. Because of the school-to-prison pipeline. Because school is about more than memorization. Because childhood is something to be honored and preserved. Because there's only a short period of time to spend with our children, and why send them away all day? Because, because, because.

This list reflects our country's cavernous divisions. At the same time, homeschooling is a peculiar prism through which to understand societal divides. For though homeschooling families' reservations about institutional education reflect varying political beliefs, the families all arrive at an identical solution: educate children at home. But doing so only promises further stratification. What does it say about the US education system that so many people are opting out, and how did we get here?

School as we know it in this country is a relatively new concept. Prior to colonization, Indigenous groups learned within their families and close-knit communities, and from their elders. The same was largely true of the Europeans who invaded this land. In colonial America, education tended to take place in the household, as many homeschoolers like to point out, but also, formally and informally, in the world: in the fields where children labored, in the homes of their friends and community leaders, in places of worship and of work. As Jana Harcharek, an Indigenous leader working for the North Slope Borough School District in Alaska, once put it to me, "There's a difference between education and schooling."

But over time, school—an institutional setting implementing a standardized curriculum and learning format—emerged as the primary mechanism through which our country's children were supposed to learn. Today's US public education system evolved from a few different philosophies in early America. The Common Schools Movement of the Revolutionary era was one of them—it held that education was a fundamental pillar of democracy. Its leaders, including Thomas Jefferson, argued that "the survival of the young republic depended upon educated citizens who could understand public issues, who would elect virtuous leaders, and who would sustain the delicate balance between liberty and order in the new political system." Later, in the mid-nineteenth century, "charity schools" began conscripting the poor children of the country's growing cities into schools. These schools were exclusively for the poor, and were focused less on academics than on "moral education." As Sheila Curran Bernard and Sarah Mondale put it in *School: The Story of American Public Education*, the charity schools "treated poverty as a defect of character." Education reformers of that era, they write, "denigrated the charity

schools for isolating the poor, but they admired the highly organized urban systems that had evolved from them." These were the precursors to today's large school districts.

But the shift toward a compulsory, national public school system took time. Voters (not unlike today's homeschoolers) feared government intervention in education and schooling, particularly those in rural and religious communities. Reformers like Horace Mann, who saw education as "the great equalizer of the conditions of men—the balance-wheel of the social machinery," campaigned for universal, secular education taught by well-trained teachers; other reformers like Emma Willard and Catharine Beecher campaigned for female education. All of them believed school should be available to children at no

cost, and should be funded by tax dollars. Horace Mann was appointed the first education secretary of Massachusetts. Later, in 1852, the state became the first in the nation to require its children to attend school. By 1860, most states had created a superintendent of schools position dedicated to formalizing and standardizing a common education system, and by 1918, school was compulsory in every state in the Union. The reformers had been successful. Education was now widely, if not exclusively, viewed as both a social lever and a public good that allowed for the ascent and well-being of the individual, but also the ascent and well-being of the nation.

This lofty ideal of education, as it is both obvious but necessary to emphasize, was applied only to white boys, and sometimes to white girls. And it is thus no surprise that school in this country has also long functioned as an agent of violence and repression. Starting in the late nineteenth century, tens of thousands of Indigenous children were forced into state-run boarding schools, where they were separated from their families, compelled to do manual labor, beaten for speaking their native languages, and physically and sexually abused. These schools were responsible for the deaths of at least five hundred children, according to a recent federal report, but probably many more. Their campuses were littered with mass graves, where the bodies of children who died in the schools' care were hidden away.

Such endemic violence is not a mere vestige of schools past. The chance that a Black child attends a high-poverty school is more than double that of a white child. Not unlike the mission of the charity schools of yore, the mission of some educators still seems to be to "civilize" Black and brown children into the norms of a white-dominated society. Though Black children account for only 16 percent of students enrolled in public school, they account for 31 percent of school-related arrests, according to the ACLU, and are suspended and expelled three times as often as white students—and those who have been suspended or expelled are three times as likely to end up in the juvenile justice system. What has been called "the school-to-prison pipeline" ensures that poor Black and brown students in certain districts are more likely to end up in prison than they are to go to college.

Education as a public good remains an elusive fantasy, yet is it not an ideal worth fighting for? "The road necessarily traveled to achieve freedom and equality in the United States leads directly through public education," writes Dr. Noliwe Rooks in the introduction to her book *Cutting School: The Segrenomics of American Education*. Throughout this country's history, white supremacists have tried to keep Black people, as well as immigrants, Natives, Asians, and brown people, from enjoying equitable public education opportunities—or sometimes any school at all. It has always been clear to white supremacists as well as to those in power that going to school is a mechanism of upward mobility. ("Education," as lawyer and diplomat J.L.M. Curry put it to the Alabama General Assembly in 1889, "would spoil a good plowhand.")

At the same time, education is big business. Free, universal access to our public education system is already hobbled by charters and private schools that, in the name of school choice, siphon off both resources and students from the public system. Virtual and homeschool charters are the next for-profit frontier. These schools, based overwhelmingly in poor Black and brown districts, recruit students by promising excellence and an alternative path from the standard "failing" public schools. Unlike in typical charter schools, all coursework happens online, and, in spite of having no buildings to maintain or non-teaching staff, like attendance clerks and food service workers, some are reimbursed by the state at the same per-pupil rate. To lure students, they even advertise on TV channels like Nickelodeon and the Cartoon Network. "Such schools are neither effective nor inexpensive," writes Rooks, "yet they continue to expand"— even more so post-pandemic, when fewer people are sending their children back to school.

Freedom of choice and the open market are fundamental to the American way—and so, it seems, is a fear of government interference in our children's education. "We can go to the mall and buy whatever we want," writes Sam Blumenfeld in a 2000 article in *Practical Homeschooling*. "But when it comes to education, suddenly we are confronted with compulsory school attendance laws, compulsory property taxes to pay for the government schools, compulsory testing, compulsory inoculations, forced busing, restrictions against prayer, forced sex ed, death ed, and drug ed."

In most states it's easy enough for a family to register as a homeschool— it requires just a bit of initial paperwork and periodic progress reports. A number of national homeschool agencies help parents navigate the process. However righteous the reason for opting to homeschool, the choice can be seen as the ultimate act of privatization: creating a school of one.

What is school for? Is school a mechanism for amassing knowledge or for learning to navigate the world? Is school meant to prepare a child for life or for further school? Is it fundamentally a social endeavor—a society in miniature? Or is it a place to get one's wider social-emotional needs met, like mental health and public benefits— a place to be safe and to be fed? Is it a place for students to bask in the innocence of childhood or meet the realities of the world? To expand their horizons or protect them? Is school a place for a person to discover who they are, and equip them to better become that person? Or is school an economic equalizer and a lever of democracy?

A school is shaped by how the people running it (or funding it) answer the question of school's fundamental purpose, and central to the problem of education in this country is that we can no longer agree on the answer—if we ever could. Given this fact, along with the rot at the center of school's history and the profit set to be made by alternatives to public school, it is no wonder that the system is falling apart—and that more and more people are pulling out altogether.

hen Sofia was in middle school in New York City, her teachers never called on her. There were racist incidents all the time—students calling her the N-word, students bullying her for her looks—and Sofia, who is Puerto Rican, never felt her teachers did a good job intervening. She was sometimes harassed on the way to school. She'd harbored great anxiety in the classroom and school hallways ever since she was a little kid: about grades, about having the right answers, about doing the right thing, about generally acting right. Then, in the spring of 2019, her mom, Alyssa, got a job in California, and so Sofia, Alyssa, and Sofia's two siblings moved. When COVID hit, Sofia and her siblings were on Zoom all day long. She felt extra anxiety being on camera, as if everyone were watching her.

When online school reopened the next fall, Sofia and her siblings enrolled in public school, but by October they'd had enough and opted back into homeschooling. Alyssa felt it was better for her kids to be self-directed and engaged in what and how they were learning, and on schedules that better suited their adolescent biorhythms. But the pressure on her as a parent was immense. She was trying to keep up with three separate curricula—essentially, trying to replicate the school experience, but at home. She joined some Facebook groups in search of support, but the communities she found were largely right-wing, religious, and/or conservative, which didn't match Alyssa's ethics. The other parents in these forums were also mostly white. But then she found a group called My Reflection Matters, which was made up largely of women of color dedicated to the notions of conscious parenting and "unschooling"—a philosophy taking hold throughout the country, in which children learn with limited structure and based on their own interests and at their own pace.

"I was like, This clicks and this makes sense to me," Alyssa told me. It dawned on her that our educational system just told people what to learn and how to learn it. No wonder so many people ended up lost. She wanted her kids to recognize what excited them. She realized it just wasn't possible to replicate school at home—nor did she want to. Effective homeschooling meant shedding the rigidity of institutional school. It also meant building special relationships with one's kids and an open line of communication. Once this paradigm was revealed to her, the entire family relaxed—and began loving homeschooling more than they had ever loved actual school.

Sofia, in particular, relished learning at home. She signed up for classes through an Agile Learning Center—an increasingly popular distance-learning platform which allows students to sign up for short learning modules on anything from basket weaving to video game design. She loved fashion and period costumes, so she began helping out as a period performer at her local historical center. One day she just marched over there and asked for an internship. They'd never had an intern before, but they were impressed by Sofia's initiative. They made a role for her.

"Now Sofia and I talk way more than we ever did, because there's not this authoritative [dynamic of], *You have to do it this way*," Alyssa told me. Wouldn't most consider hers a successful learning experience? A student engaged in her work and better prepared to meet the world? Alyssa says she is just the facilitator, making sure Sofia has what she needs.

Homeschooling also allowed Sofia to better understand herself. A few months into homeschooling, she diagnosed herself as autistic. Alyssa dismissed her at first, but the more they looked into it together, the more it seemed to track. It explained some of her debilitating anxiety. Neither her autism nor her anxiety was supported or seen in the school context; at home, she could make choices to manage them.

Alyssa and her kids feel liberated. And there are many who understand homeschooling writ large—and unschooling in particular—as liberation work. School, after all, is a vestige of colonization. A rapidly growing demographic of homeschoolers are Black families and other families of color who have been failed—or expect to be failed—by institutional education.

"Instead of trying to work within the system to lobby and hope for change," writes writer and unschooling advocate Akilah Richards, who leads the Raising Free People Network, "we are designing our own liberation."

Many critics point out the luxury of homeschooling, but Richards contends that by shifting priorities, anyone can do it. She and her partner have two school-aged kids. "Today," she writes, "our measure of success ignores GPAs, degrees and the American Dream, and instead puts a focus on confident autonomy, autodidactic learning, strong discernment skills and happy people who are willing to approach their own ideas of liberation and joy…"

This utopic, liberatory framework for education seems to be taking hold nationwide. "What do I want to center here?" asked Frieda, a white homeschooling parent of two in Western Massachusetts, of her own unschooling practice when we spoke this spring. "I want them to know how to heal themselves." She is a dancer turned herbalist, and her children help her mix her tinctures and light the yurt's woodstove before her sessions.

"I want them to know how to make a fire without a match. I want them to listen to birdsong and sit in the woods and pay attention. To sit not just in a place of doing, but [of] being receptive." She paused. "I want to create a place of receptiveness." She sees the devastation of the planet, and the crushing inequality facing the world, as stemming from the lack of such attunement. By slowing her whole family down, helping them connect to the earth and to their wider community, she feels they'll be better stewards and people. In her eyes, this is

best fostered outside the rigid confines of traditional school: at home.

I spoke to another homeschooler, named Bethany, who lives in Marin County, across the bay from my home in Berkeley, California. Her kid is fourteen and was homeschooling before the pandemic. She explained that homeschool "gives people freedom of choice no matter what freedom they want." It's not always about the curriculum, she points out, but sometimes about the other trappings of school: the schedule, the commute, the social pressures, the mandatory vaccines.

During the early pandemic, more and more people in her town were opting to homeschool. Bethany helped form a small network of families so kids could rotate between houses to study and to play. This network grew and more parents contacted her, hoping to join. At the beginning of the 2022–23 school year, they had eighteen kids in their group from throughout Marin County—too many to host at a single home. And the kids needed a bit more structure too.

So Bethany's group found a building to rent four days a week. It was an old log cabin built by the local veterans' society; the upstairs, where the homeschoolers began to meet, functioned as a community center, and downstairs was a low-lit bar where local vets gathered to drink. They arranged sixth-, seventh-, and eighth-grade pods. One of the parents signed up to teach science. Another offered to teach Shakespeare. A recently retired teacher from Bolinas had some extra time on his hands; they hired him to teach math and science. Another teacher, who had recently left his public school district after more

than a decade, became the social studies teacher. During lunchtime, students ate at the play structure. They were asked to give up their cell phones each morning to avoid distractions. Each day of the week, a different homeschool parent was in charge of keeping things running smoothly—not unlike, say, a principal.

The homeschool pod had created something together, and what they'd created looked and functioned remarkably like a school. The only difference was that it was a school made in the image and values of the parents sending their kids there.

I arranged to visit on a particularly hot spring day. I'd come in time to observe a science class taught by one of the dads, which was meeting out back in the shade of redwoods, by a creek still running with the spoils of high winter rains. The teacher-dad gathered the students around a table. Each pair had been given a different experiment to conduct, and now they were re-creating the experiments for the group and explaining the chemical reactions taking place. I watched as a trio deposited a stack of Mentos into a two-liter bottle of Coke, which immediately began fizzing over with foam. "Pay attention!" the teacher-dad encouraged over the chatter. Besides being outdoors, the class looked more or less like a regular science class in a regular school, but with far fewer students: something was being learned, and a teacher was redirecting students toward the task at hand.

I walked back around to the front of the school, where Bethany and Amy, the parents on duty, sat in the sun. Amy's sixth- and eighth-grade daughters were attending this school. She explained that she had opted to take her girls out of

the district because she wanted her children to learn according to their family's values. This echoed what many homeschooling parents had told me, and made sense. I knew that when the time came for my daughter to go to school I, too, would want her to attend a school that aligned with my values. But I also recognized the perils of this line of thinking. It suggested that a value system is static and absolute, and it left little room for a child to learn beyond the reaches of what her parents believed.

I asked Amy what the values were that most guided her family, and that she most worried her children weren't learning at their public school. She cocked her head and thought about this for a minute. "Huh, I'm trying to think," she said. Values weren't always an easy thing to articulate—they were sometimes more felt than spoken.

It was far easier to articulate the reverse: the values one felt were being imposed on their children at school. For instance: "You know, going into the whole gender issue." She paused. "That's one of those things where you're like, I don't really know how I feel about that. I don't have anything against it, per se, but when it's pushed on my kids, that's when I feel like I'm not quite sure."

Of course, parents push ideas onto their children all the time, and children are constantly barraged by ideological forces outside the home: from teachers, yes, but also from their peers, from the advertisements they see on TV or social media, from faith groups and soccer coaches and people at the grocery store or the playground. It's only when such ideas don't match our own ways of thinking that parents balk. And if Amy felt that the "gender issue"

(which I took to mean the wider inclusion of trans-accepting language and practices at school) were being pushed on her children, someone else (me, for instance) might see it differently: that, by deciding to keep her child out of an environment where they were learning about the gender spectrum, a mother might be denying that child access to a worldview that both created a more caring environment and better reflected an opening world.

Parents make all sorts of decisions, for better and for worse, about what their children can access and do. The notion that we can insulate and isolate our children from what we see as nefarious forces strikes me as both the fundamental work of parenting and also the wild hubris of it. For this notion presupposes that it is even *possible* to protect our children from ideas and influences we don't agree with. It also presumes that the parents' worldview is both correct and complete, and that we can supply our children with all the information they need to live their lives.

At the same time, I harbored the same preoccupations as a parent. I understood that it was far easier for me to be clear-eyed about the perils of hegemonic value systems when the values at hand—trans acceptance, for instance—were in line with my own. What if my life's circumstances dictated that my family and I live in Florida, say, where anyone can carry a gun without a permit, and where state curriculum standards are now essentially teaching that Rosa Parks was merely a tired lady on a bus? In such a case, I knew, my belief that children should be exposed to value systems outside

MY DOCTOR WARNS ME AGAINST TRAVEL ABROAD
or **WHAT IS A DREAM TO ME**

by Camille Rankine

To grieve
an American grief

a delicate feeling:
from afar   wistful

and brief   To grow soft
on the milk of America   thick

with its sleep   To export its
ruin   outspend its disease

To live in a house with death
in its walls   bent-backed

in its building   to wander its halls
vigilant in the dark

To be born in the hold
of this dream   burnt black in its glare

pick the fruit from its tree
turn its fruits in my hands   leave the bruised

to their rot   take my choice
cut of meat

To be shaped by a day
lived long

before me   a long dead thing
that visits my sleep

now a thing to forget:
An American grief

---

those of their parents would swiftly turn to dust.

Even while working inside the school machine, I'd long grappled with both the meaning and the purpose of school. Though I'd been a school administrator for over a decade, I'd often harbored the feeling that what we try to improve about schools—the curriculum, the teacher training, the test scores—is somewhat beside the point. Yes, it matters what we learn, but far more important is *how* we learn it. And the important learning that happens in schools, to my eye, has always been more social in nature. We learn to live and work in community. We learn to organize our thoughts and share them. We learn to listen to and interpret the thoughts of others. We learn deadlines and consequences, and to be beholden to a group. We learn hierarchies and, depending on the nature of the learning environment, how to perpetuate or question these divisions and exclusions. And we learn how to learn.

A few things became clear during the pandemic closures. One was that school was a vital form of child care, and that without it, parents could not do their own jobs. Another was that distance learning only exacerbated existing inequalities: parents in working-class jobs had less flexibility in their schedules to accommodate their children and help them in school, and poor families lacked the critical infrastructure—laptops, internet connections—needed for online learning. Another thing that became clear was that not a lot of learning happened via online learning—perhaps because so many of the social elements I listed above had been stripped away.

The school I worked at served newly arrived immigrant English language learners from around the world, and over 95 percent of our students lived at or below the poverty line. When our school shuttered for in-person learning in March of 2020, few students had a laptop at home, even fewer had an internet connection, and almost none had both. Many of our students and their family members worked in restaurants that had closed, leaving them, suddenly and devastatingly, with no income. So we spent those early months of the pandemic creating phone trees, signing up students for internet service, and doling out donated computers (masked, with gloves on) to students' homes. We also signed up families for emergency unemployment and arranged food-delivery systems so families had something to eat. It was demanding and urgent work—but it also highlighted what I had always suspected to be the truth of education: that schools are just as meaningful, if not more so, because of what happens outside the classroom, and that schools are, above all, communities—ones that both reflect and determine the functioning of society at large.

This is what made the homeschooling trends all the more worrisome to me on a larger scale, if all the more understandable.

But in a way I wasn't much unlike the new class of homeschoolers. In the fall of 2021, beaten down by the challenges of working within a system of vast dysfunction, I left my job of nearly fifteen years.

In those early days of mass shutdowns, there was a small flicker of a silver lining: perhaps, with everything having ground to a halt, we might be able to not just rebuild but entirely reimagine what school could look like. The same was true of other failing social systems: equitable health care, cities and public spaces that prioritized walking and biking, and a robust social safety net all felt

like priorities that might flourish in the wake of the COVID catastrophe. There was an opportunity to start anew. But one of the secondary tragedies of the pandemic is that, when it comes to these critical social systems, it failed to induce meaningful structural change. After in-person learning returned, school looked just like it had before, only with COVID tests and handwashing stations and some feeble attempts at social distancing.

I wasn't the only one leaving. Prior to the pandemic, 75 percent of states were reckoning with a teacher shortage—for people were both leaving the profession and failing to join. By 2022, there was a 3.1 percent teacher vacancy rate—one of the highest rates ever. Administrators were tired. Teachers were burned-out, and once school resumed, the work was even more demanding. Class sizes weren't smaller. The students were behind after so much learning loss, and were struggling with mental health. Andrew, the teacher at the log cabin school who left his district job, told me that he and his fellow teachers had to use the passing periods between classes to sanitize their classrooms, and no new custodians were hired to help. When were teachers supposed to eat a snack or pee?

"Things were out of control," he said, and there weren't enough resources—or even enough will—to meet the need. "There was all that lip service when we were on Zoom of, like, *Oh my god, we realize how valuable teachers are, now we're going to make changes*," Andrew told me. "I realized that I'd been fighting for change in the public education system [for years]. And if the pandemic didn't actually

make any significant change, then it's never gonna happen."

This was, in part, what made me leave my job: the feeling that I, and the rest of us public educators, would be rolling the same damn rock uphill for the rest of our lives.

eaving public education offered me a break, but it didn't satisfy my desire for answers about what school was for, or how the disintegrating schooling system might be rectified. So one afternoon last spring, I dropped my daughter at her grandfather's house and drove out to Bolinas, California, a sleepy beach town perched on the continent's edge, to meet a woman named Rasa. She was an unschooling mother of three and pregnant with her fourth. She, her partner, and her kids traveled the country in a ramshackle blue van— a "gypsy clan," as she put it, "raising the vibe by redistributing health and wealth."

I met Rasa and her three kids at the beach. It was a particularly warm day, and her children—ages two, three, and six—soon stripped down naked and tumbled around in the sand. Rasa explained that in her twenties, she'd had a spiritual awakening that caused her to leave her job and marriage for the open road. She'd come to see that capital drove everything and corrupted both human relationships and the earth. She didn't want anything to do with those systems anymore, so she wandered in search of another way. She worked on organic farms in exchange for room and board

and regularly attended Rainbow Gatherings—events in the woods where participants cook, sing, and dance together. She hadn't been sure she'd have kids, but her partner—whom she'd met at a Rainbow Gathering—said, "But if not us, who?" Parenting became an extension of her attempts to live in a paradigm outside capital and greed. And their school—or lack thereof—would be a part of this paradigm.

Rasa's three-year-old sat in the sand, making an imaginary birthday cake. "Happy birthday to Mommy!" he sang, handing a piece of this cake to Rasa, which she pretend-gobbled eagerly while her two-year-old leaped into her arms to nurse.

Rasa was happy to be on the beach that day, but she also seemed exhausted. She admitted it was much

harder to live a non-normative life, and harder and harder with each new kid. She was around seven months pregnant (she forgoes institutional medical care in favor of what's known as "freebirth") and chasing after three little ones. Any structure that held her children was up to her to forge. That morning, the three of them had been particularly squirrely and her partner was working a short-term construction gig, leaving her to parent alone. She'd thought of calling me to cancel our meeting.

"Sometimes I feel like an impostor," she told me. "Like it would just be easier to vaccinate these kids and send them to school."

But as a brown woman with brown children, she didn't want any part in a schooling system that had been a function of empire and genocide.

Becoming a mother was a chance to decolonize herself and her children. "I want to be able to nurture them to learn what they want to learn. I want them to be as sovereign as possible and gaining what I think public school lacks: emotional intelligence."

What my conversation with Rasa put into stark relief is that homeschooling both reflects and presages a larger dynamic of distrust in this country's institutions and public promises—which I tended to share, in my own ways and with my own interpretations. American individualism makes clear that it's up to you to make your own life—and capitalism makes clear that there's no guarantee that anyone or anything will support you as you do it.

I had a neighbor once, on a quiet hill above the UC Berkeley campus, who began homeschooling her young daughter, Nymue. I followed them on Instagram: Nymue collecting herbs from the hillside to make tea, Nymue dancing on the beach, Nymue at a many-day silent meditation retreat in India.

"Giving children a space of love and a trusting environment to explore from is some of the most sacred work we can do," Bronwyn, her mother, wrote. "I want to prepare Nymue to live an extraordinary life—to do what it is she came here to do, to enjoy the incredible opportunity of being alive, to be kind and embodied. I want her to have the opportunity to shape herself into herself."

Like with Rasa and many of the homeschooling parents I spoke with, I was struck by Bronwyn's commitment and clarity of purpose. It sounded so beautiful. And I wanted what she described for my daughter too.

Often, parents spoke about the desire to slow down and savor time with their children—to savor time in general. "I love my children," one influential homeschool podcaster told me. "I think they are amazing people and I like spending time with them." Though I was awed by these parents' resolve (even if I didn't always agree with their politics), it was also true that I did not really want to spend all day, every day—or even all day *most* days—with my child. This was hard to admit, especially as I had more conversations with people who did.

"I've thought about how maybe it's particularly hard to become a parent when you were happy with your life," I wrote to a friend while in the midst of researching this article. My friend had also recently had a baby and was struggling, like I had, with the swallowing nature of early parenthood. "Like, I didn't have a child because I had some gaping hole to fill, or because I couldn't imagine my life without one. I loved my life! But I did want a child." What I meant was that I didn't see these days with my child as my glory days, as the homeschooling folk duo had put it on the opening night of Wild + Free. Rather, I wanted all the days—what came before my child, what came now as a new parent, and all that was to come—to be as glorious as possible. And for me, that would require my daughter to be elsewhere at times. Like at school.

But there was another, more moral dimension to my desire to engage in the formal education system: I felt a responsibility, as a white parent, to invest in public education by sending my daughter to a public school. I wanted what Bronwyn described for my own child, yes—but I wanted this for all children too. Statistically, I know my kid will be fine no matter where she goes, be it a low-performing California public school, the popular bilingual magnet school, a forest school, a private school, or unschooling in my backyard. If I spent the majority of my time concocting the best, most individualized experience for my white kid, I would, at the end, be fomenting and perpetuating inequality. I don't judge the other parents I spoke to—especially the parents of color—who opt out of public school, but I can't imagine choosing against it when the time comes. It worries me that many white parents start off with my same convictions, but end up changing their mind when the rubber meets the road.

"I mean, sometimes I feel bad, I feel selfish," Bethany said of her choice to homeschool her kid (she herself is an intervention teacher in a public school). But on the other hand, she felt that the more people choose another path, the more change can be seeded. "I think people forget that they have a lot of fucking power," she said. "They can make choices." The more people choose another way, in her eyes, the more large-scale change might occur for all. And others, like Akilah Richards, saw it far more bluntly: that equality will never emerge from public schools and must be found elsewhere—starting by learning at home and in the wider world.

All the while, I'd been asking the question, What is school for? But in fact, that was the privatized, individuated version of the question I was really after. What I really wanted to know was, What is a public education system for?

There are elements of homeschooling—and particularly of unschooling—that appeal to me deeply both as a parent and as an educator, particularly the notions that schools should be freer of the structures and constraints that limit children, and that students will learn better if guided by their own instincts and wonder. But I also believe in—and am committed to—the value of an accessible, equal, public system. How might it be possible to have both? Homeschooling doesn't just presage the end of school—it also offers insights into how to fix it. Sometimes the fringe has something to teach us about what is missing in the mainstream.

Right after my daughter was born, I agreed to return to work at the school I'd left the year prior. It was a small contract, for only a couple hours a week, but I was back. I'd missed the work of building and imagining an ever-better school. I hadn't missed the overwhelm and jadedness that often accompanied it. But what if I harnessed the sense of optimism, wonder, and joy that Wild + Free trafficked in, and that was shared by so many homeschoolers I talked to across the political spectrum?

So I'm back to rolling the rock uphill again and again. But maybe what the homeschoolers were showing me was that it was foolish to keep trying to tip the rock over to the other side. What if we spent more energy at the base of the hill—that is, remaking the world where we already live? ✶

ANNIE-B PARSON

[CHOREOGRAPHER, DANCER]

"DANCE DOESN'T HAVE ANY OF ITS OWN MEANING.
IT MEANS WHAT YOU MAKE IT MEAN."

A few of Annie-B Parson's favorite verbs:

To walk

To divine

To disassemble

To detach

To lay

More or less, I found myself at David Byrne's American Utopia *by accident. I had tagged along with my mother, who had announced she was coming to town for the express purpose of seeing it, and I arrived at the theater knowing nothing other than that it was David Byrne's musical. Halfway through the second number, I was fumbling for my program. Who had made this choreography? It was unusual for a Broadway show: pedestrian and precise, unshowy, sometimes awkward—but satisfyingly so. This dancing looked more like it belonged in Judson Memorial Church, the seat of the downtown experimental dance scene in New York, than in a Broadway theater. I found my program under my seat: Oh, of course. Annie-B Parson.*

Parson has been a luminary of the New York City dance and theater scene since the early '90s, when she formed Big Dance Theater with director Paul Lazar (also her husband) and performer Molly Hickok. She did indeed come out of the Judson scene, and was influenced by its avant-garde sensibility. After seeing the work of German dancer Pina Bausch at age twenty-five, she also began to incorporate classical theatrical modes of storytelling into her work: character, costume, certain forms of plot. Big Dance Theater productions are ambitious works of formal and intellectual omnivorousness. Her 2021 work, The Mood Room, featured contemporary German house music, a narrative thread about 1980s Los Angeles and Reaganism, Chekhov's Three Sisters, soap operas, and the Gnostic Gospels. Other recurring inspirations: ancient Greek tragedies, the Old Testament, braided hair, Thoreau, Kabuki, Russian folk dancing, classical ballet, and so on.

Parson's work as a choreographer has also extended beyond her own company, and particularly into collaborations with musicians. American Utopia is only one part of a years-long collaboration with Byrne: she choreographed his Love This Giant tour with St. Vincent and his musical Here Lies Love, which opened on Broadway in the summer of 2023. She has collaborated with David Bowie, Anne Carson, Laurie Anderson, Lorde, Salt-N-Pepa, and plenty of others. The Martha Graham Dance Company has two large-scale works of hers in its repertory.

During the pandemic, Parson began writing a book—one unlike the books she had previously written, which include an illustrated abecedary titled Dance by Letter, and Drawing the Surface of Dance: A Biography in Charts, for which she drew her dances as illustrations, mapping their graphic structures. Her latest book, The Choreography of Everyday Life (Verso Books, 2022), documents the early months of the pandemic and serves as a record of her creative philosophy. It proposes that choreography is everywhere, in our most basic personal and civic routines, suffused in the world around us. Equally, it shows the way Parson allows the world around her (from gestures to iPhone photographs to Greek tragedy) to suffuse her own work. The book delighted me—with its ideas about creative process and its prose rhythms, which mimic dance rhythms—so I asked Parson if we could talk about it.

We met at her home in Brooklyn, New York. The night before, I'd gone to the Brooklyn Academy of Music (BAM) to see a restaging of Água, the 2001 evening-length work by Pina Bausch, which Parson had also recently seen. In anticipation of our talk, she'd just looked at The Choreography of Everyday Life for the first time in months. We spent about an hour and a half at her kitchen table, snacking on a lemon cake and talking about the ephemerality of dance, the Gnostic Gospels, and kinesthetic empathy.

—Jordan Kisner

I. THE ROLODEX OF THE DANCER

THE BELIEVER: You looked again at your book this morning.

ANNIE-B PARSON: Yes.

BLVR: How was that?

ABP: It was fine, but the photos are too dark, and I'd forgotten that. It jumped out at me that something I was doing in the book but didn't quite realize is that the book's also about sound. I know it's about space, I know it's about time, I know it's about proximity and duality and all these elements of Theater—capital-T Theater. But I guess I didn't really take in how much it's got sound. *I can't hear this, because the radio's on*, or *I can't hear this, because the AC's on*, or *Oh, I* heard *this*, or *I* heard *it because the window's open*. Oh, I heard *that Trump was elected through the window*. That *should have a sound cue*, or *That* shouldn't *have a sound cue*. I didn't realize this.

BLVR: Right. Is there a reason that's top of mind for you right now? Sound in particular?

ABP: No, I don't think so. I think I just needed to have some separation from the book to see how present it was.

BLVR: That makes sense. When you say that, I'm like, Oh, of course, it's in there—but it wasn't the first, or second, or third thing that I noticed in the book either.

ABP: If I was sound—if I could personify sound—I'd be like, *Nobody pays attention to me!* You go to a theater piece and sometimes I have 150 sound cues in my work. And nobody ever mentions it. And they're so significant. They define what you're looking at. In straight theater, they tell you how to feel.

BLVR: Or because there's so much else… Especially in the

realm of theater and dance, there's so much other stimulation happening, often, that it fades into—

ABP: And that's cultural, don't you think? For instance, we're very geared toward paying attention to language. I am not, personally. I am narratively challenged. I'm not following the text. I'm looking at and listening to sound cues—the way they use space. I'm looking at it like a choreographer. I can't help it. I'm not even trying to.

BLVR: That's interesting because one of the things that I've been picking up as I've gone through your work is actually how much you seem attuned to language. How language seems so primary for you.

ABP: Absolutely. It is. But not narrative.

BLVR: You've said in the past something I'm really obsessed with, which is that our body is like a memory organ: it carries everything that's ever happened to us. But also, movement of the body, and dance in particular, are so ephemeral. How do you think about memory in relation to your work and in relation to your practice? It feels like the body is this memory organ but the thing that results from it can't be held, or can only be held in memory. How do you feel about that?

ABP: It's an upsetting subject, because there's no… Dance is so ephemeral that I have no record of my work, basically. Like, the experience that you have watching a live piece is, of course, unrelated to watching something at the library. And that experience of you in relation to the work is what I'm interested in. Only every once in a while have I been able to have that experience with a video… That's why *American Utopia* was such a big deal for me. Because Spike Lee came in with thirteen cameras and he said, "I want to follow the choreography." [Spike Lee directed and produced a 2020 concert film of a Broadway performance of *American Utopia*.] So that's a real record of that piece. I'd never thought in my whole life that I'd have a real record of my work. And I hate ephemerality. And I don't romanticize it.

It's a very odd, fleeting, embodied experience when you leave a dance performance. It's in you, as a viewer, but it's not like how you can go to the Met your whole life and look at a Vermeer. You can't. You can't reexperience it the way I can

reexperience the Old Testament every weekend. I can reexperience the Bible, if I take the time! I didn't today. [*Laughs*] I can't do that with dance.

BLVR: That also means you can't track the way you change in relation to the art. We *do* pay attention to how books read to us through different decades or how we see a painting differently.

ABP: That's very important! That's the triangle I talk about in my book. You, the book, the world. You, the dance, the world. We can't do that with dance. Unless someone like BAM brings a twenty-year-old Pina Bausch piece [*Água*] with seventy-five people… Seventy-five people were on tour for that. Imagine the resources. Did you see that piece?

BLVR: I just saw it last night. It was… spectacular.

ABP: Yes. It's remarkable. And you can imagine, like, that's one piece we get to see, not just from Pina Bausch, but from many choreographers. It's so rare. And that piece is only twenty years old. What about a piece that's one hundred and twenty years old? So yeah, dance is fucked. It's just gone. It just goes. It just keeps going away. And some people think that's cool. I don't.

BLVR: To what extent is that a problem you feel like you can intervene in?

ABP: Book!

BLVR: Right.

ABP: That's it. Just the book. Because my happiest thing about the book is it never closes. It doesn't have a two-week run, or a three-day run. You know what I mean? Anyone can read it. Anytime, forever. This book thing is *good*. I'm just like, This makes sense.

BLVR: That it becomes something that can exist, or that can persist in time.

ABP: Persist, and that you can revisit. And see who you are in relation to it, or to any book.

BLVR: The other thing I'm thinking of is that the closest analogue to that is in the bodies of longtime collaborators.

ABP: The Rolodex of the dancer. Absolutely.

BLVR: They can hold some of that.

ABP: They do. And I do. The few dancers that hold huge amounts of information in their bodies, of my work—I can't even tell you how I feel about them. They're literally walking repositories.

BLVR: They're your archive.

ABP: They're my archive. And of course, I'm at their whim, basically. They have so much power for me. And the way that material has been internalized—and I'm talking about a very small handful of people—with them is so beautiful, the work they hold. I have two dancers that literally have, like, twenty years of movement in their bodies.

BLVR: What an unbelievable relationship between two people.

ABP: It's intense.

BLVR: I wonder if they feel this way about it, but it seems like a lot of pressure on them.

ABP: It's a lot of power for them. And I hope it's not pressure. I hope they feel like they're the goods. They have the currency—I hope. Yeah. I don't think they feel pressure.

BLVR: I guess the reason I thought of the word *pressure* is because sometimes I work on projects that involve archives. Like literal paper archives. And often it seems like the people whose job it is to maintain those archives feel a kind of obligation, that this is a precious thing they are stewarding.

ABP: I hope they feel that way.

BLVR: I mean, I wonder. To feel like in my body is this thing that doesn't really exist anywhere else.

ABP: That's absolutely the case. I know there was this famous reconstruction of the 1913 version of *The Rite of Spring* and there was a woman—I think her name was Millicent Hodson. She had retained that material in her body and was very old, and the Joffrey [Ballet] put it back together, using her direction. I saw the reconstruction, like, decades ago. Of course, I had nothing to compare it to. But it was off the charts, one of the most memorable things I've ever seen. And that woman is the archive. She's carrying the sacred material. She's holding... You know, recently they found that thousand-year-old Torah. And everybody was up in arms because in the picture the person didn't have gloves on, the person holding the Torah. Did you hear about this? It was in the paper just yesterday.

BLVR: Really? I didn't see it.

ABP: *I* was one of those people. I saw the picture and I was like, Why do they have their bare hands on that Torah? When I saw the picture, I had the same freak-out. I was like, She should be wearing gloves! Why isn't she wearing gloves? It's too old, it's going to fall apart. And, no, I was completely wrong, which I love. The bare hands—the oil in our skin—is actually fine for the manuscript. What's bad is the gloves. Because it's natural. There's no mitigating material between the hand and the book. They're all a tree, in a sense. I loved that.

BLVR: In a metaphysical sense, it really satisfies me, the idea that the book wants to be touched by a human hand. It makes me think about contagion magic.

ABP: What is that?

BLVR: Contagion magic is the notion, as it manifests throughout eras and cultures, that something of a person is contained in the objects that they touched often. So, like, the theory behind a relic being holy is contagion magic.

ABP: Ohhhh!

BLVR: It's something of you that's in your sweater, or in your book. I've been thinking about it, because if we're thinking about the book that wants to be touched by a human hand, one of the things that is special about a book that's so old— like the Torah or, no, maybe the Torah is special because it's a holy book… But if you think about holding a book that was in Emily Dickinson's house, the thing that makes that book special is that she held it. That's contagion magic.

ABP: That's such a scary word for it… *contagion*.

BLVR: I know, but also magic!

ABP: That's just got to be true. It just has to be true.

II. FAITH, NOT FATE

BLVR: How do you accumulate your material? It seems like so much of your process, whether it's dance-making or writing or sketching, is collage-like. So how do you magpie your world together?

ABP: I do call myself a magpie. I think it's a belief system— which may be false and which doesn't work all the time—which is that everything is related to everything. So, like, when I did Flaubert's *A Simple Heart*, underneath that is a score of stage directions in a Chekhov play, which are completely unrelated. But I'd read the Chekhov play at the same time I was working on the Flaubert, and I was like, These stage directions are so cool! I want to choreograph them! So I used that. Dance is very, very flexible—plastic—and you can move it in any direction. Dance doesn't have any of its own meaning. It means what you make it mean.

BLVR: I want to press again on the question of how you find the things. Is it just like a random accumulation process—if *accumulate* is the right verb? Is it a lot of reading?

ABP: It's perception. It has to do with perception. That's why I have a problem with research. Because I feel like research sounds like something you're intentionally doing that's very narrow. But that word doesn't work for me at all. I'm sure it's good for other people. But for me it's more like *living*.

For instance, right now I'm reading the new translation [by Damion Searls] of the Thomas Mann short stories. Have you read it?

BLVR: I haven't.

ABP: Oh my god, it's so good! It's starting to give me thoughts. Or, like, I have a really cool dress where the seams broke, so I sort of stripped the back off the dress. Another example: I was at the dentist, near the Morgan Library and Museum, and I went into the library and they have an exhibit about the first author and the ancient Etruscan period of writing. The clothes in the exhibit are amazing. The women wore these dresses that might be leaves, but you can't tell, because they're sculptures. They also might be fabric; I don't know. But they're, like, leaf shapes… Imagine you had a dress that was just, like, layers of leaves. So great. And all the dresses have slits. I'm doing that with my next costume. I want to do things choreographically where they slide their hands into their clothes or take a part of the fabric and move the dress.

BLVR: So your research is just moving around the world.

ABP: Just moving around the world. Like, *that* interests me, *that* interests me. I like gathering. Hunter-gathering.

BLVR: I forget which interview this was, but you once corrected an interviewer who was asking about the role of fate in things coming together to make something out of these disparate elements. And you said it's not fate, but *faith*, when you are working. There are also moments in the book when you refer to art animism, with [Fernando] Pessoa, and a belief that's more like a religion, that creating is as natural as a leaf growing. We're sort of skirting that subject: the role of faith in making. How has your thinking about that—the faith question, or the belief question—changed over time? Did you always have it?

ABP: I always had it, I think. But like everything, the more you do it, the more conscious you get about what you're doing. So I think I was very free when I was younger. I was like, Oh, I love Cassandra. I'll put her in this Pinter text. Or, like, I need Andrea Dworkin to walk in… I don't know what I was thinking. But it was, Oh, *that's* interesting to me;

that interests me. I'm looking for resonance, right? So you put these two things together, and even though they seem very disparate, they're going to shine light on each other in some weird way.

Over time, I realized that what I'm doing is this: trying to find these resonances, and I seem to think it can be anything, literally. Some people call it high/low. I don't think that describes it enough. It's not just about horizontal and vertical, nor is it about culture and currency. It's really about *this*, not *that*. *This*, not *that*. That's why I think I said it's not fate; it's faith. Because fate makes it sound like stuff comes together and you accept it. It's way more active than that.

III. WHO IS A CHOREOGRAPHER?

BLVR: I wanted to ask you about writing a book from choreographic principles. I know it's been done, but I don't see it done that often, especially not right now.

ABP: Some people see it as meta, and I think in moments it is. Choreographic principles are just art principles. It was very natural for me to do. It wasn't conscious. But time is there, definitely, and rhythm, definitely, and spaces… I'm also talking about choreographic elements and how they relate to other things, like duration, for instance, vis-à-vis poetry. I think the poem I use is a ten-line poem, by Catullus, as a way to talk about the meaning of duration. I know about compositional elements. So that's what I'm going to write *with*. That's going to be my writing. Because I don't identify as a writer. In any way.

BLVR: But you are a writer.

ABP: Really? OK, thank you.

BLVR: A writer is someone who writes.

ABP: Yeah. I mean, I feel that way about dance also, so it's very generous of you to say that. I'm not sure I could say that a choreographer is someone who choreographs.

BLVR: Why not?

ABP: Because, well, I think choreography is misunderstood as a process of generating steps. So a lot of people who are choreographers are creating steps. And you see it all the time. In every pop concert, on TV, all the time. Everybody's facing forward, they're only showing their front body, they're only dancing in unison, and they're doing steps. To me, that's like this tiny corner of the painting of what choreography is. I can *hardly* see that as choreography.

BLVR: So then who is a choreographer?

ABP: I think a choreographer is someone who looks at something in an über sense choreographically. The whole space. The whole body. My most basic definition of *choreography* is the aesthetic organization of the body in space. Because if you say it's the organization of the body in space, that could be somebody who, like an engineer, would figure out where people should stand in a production line. That is *a* choreography, but I wouldn't call that person a choreographer, because there's no aesthetic. Choreography to me has to do with the larger rendering of aesthetic through the body.

MICROINTERVIEW WITH NOOR NAGA, PART VI

THE BELIEVER: What is your relationship to nonfiction? What are your influences in that genre?

NOOR NAGA: My influences are more academic. I'm not such a theory-head, but I like the meatiness and nuance of academic books compared with a lot of contemporary nonfiction, which I find so boring. I often get to the end of an essay collection and think, Well, this should have been one essay, or, We've just been circling the same idea over and over again. I feel like a lot of nonfiction just gets away with being watered-down. I can't tell if the bar is just low. I don't know what's going on there. Or maybe it's just me. I find a lot of it really, really disappointing. And I feel like it only continues to be such a successful market because people feel good about learning "information" and continuing to educate themselves—versus fiction or poetry, which feels a bit fluffy, sort of a waste of time. I tend to prefer academic books, which I find to be better written a lot of the time. ✶

BLVR: Actually, I would maybe make a similar claim about writers and writing. I know I just said that a writer is a person who writes. But I don't *actually* think that, because everyone writes. But I do think a writer is a person who uses the materiality of text and of language and the possibility of conveying ideas through text and language as a form of specific expression that is creative and exploratory.

ABP: That's a pretty good definition. And now you've got it on tape!

BLVR: [*Laughs*] And not everyone who writes a book actually does that.

ABP: That's exactly what I'm saying. Like, I don't know what the equivalent of steps is in writing, but there definitely is one. Because sometimes you go: That person isn't a writer. They had some sort of anecdotal thing that people relate to, and great. *Writing* is this other thing. Writing is conceiving. Like Beckett is conceiving of the world in a particular way and finding language to support that. And that's where it gets into that "exploration" at the end of your sentence. [Beckett] needs to invent a whole other way of using language in order to describe this larger world. That's what I mean about the über thing. It's not just sentences.

BLVR: Right now I'm teaching a class on the nonfiction collage, or the essay collage, and I have this student who came in to talk to me because she was worried about whether it was OK that she was smooshing so many different things together. Especially because she doesn't always immediately know how to explain why this math theory and that piece of art and so on—things that apparently have no relation—belong in an essay together, but they do for her. We were talking about how one way of thinking about writing an essay is as if you're inventing a container where these disparate ideas can sit together and make sense to the reader the way they intuitively do to you, the writer.

ABP: Would you say that my book is a collage essay?

BLVR: Yeah, probably.

ABP: OK. So the way I did that, from my perspective, is through form. Like I created a form that could hold this braid structure. How would you do that?

BLVR: For me, the challenge is understanding, surfacing, what those connections are so I can actually understand them. Because often the thing that's bringing these things together feels random, and maybe even *is* a little random, but it does have a logic that's either in the ether or buried somewhere deep in my brain. And the first task is figuring out why they belong together, to me.

ABP: I've never thought about it like that.

IV. "DESCRIBE, DESCRIBE, DESCRIBE"

ABP: My very, very favorite writer right now is Isaac Babel.

BLVR: I don't know who that is—who is that?

ABP: Isaac Babel was a little after Chekhov. He was killed by Stalin. He was Jewish. He's like Chekhov with blood running down his face. Babel has a thing that I've printed out and put by my desk and it says, *Describe, describe, describe.* He says, *Describe a Cossack. Describe his pants. Describe his shoes. Describe the earth under his shoes.* And on and on and on and on. He just goes, *Describe, describe, describe.* And then he goes on to say, *Describe these very ineffable things. Describe a thunderstorm.* Things like that.

BLVR: Is there an equivalent in dance?

ABP: Oh yeah.

BLVR: What is it?

ABP: [*Exasperated sound*] Choreography is so hard. [*Laughter*] The equivalent… When you generate movement material, you then have to make it legible or repeatable, because it's never existed before—it's not like I'm working within a tradition of jazz or ballet, where there are terms. So you have to generate movement material, you have to make it legible, and you have to figure out how it moves. *Does* it move? What are its tonalities? Shaping and sculpting that material is, I guess, *describe, describe, describe*. Something like that. It's very hard. I don't even like thinking about it. [*Laughs*]

BLVR: In your first book, you write, "C is for choreography, the most unfree of forms." Why work in an unfree form, and what is a free form?

ABP: I was working with some musicians, and as I was choreographing them they were pushing back, and they said, *When we play music, we're always dancing and we feel so free and now we don't feel good.* And I was like, *Choreography isn't free. It's not free. There's nothing free about it.* It's an unfree form in that once it exists, the body is, in a sense, confined to a series of actions in a particular space in a particular time wearing particular clothes, you know what I mean? It's very unfree. What you do within it, if you're a great dancer, is very free. Like, I've seen people do things with my choreography that were thrilling. And they didn't change the choreography; they just interpreted it, lived inside it.

BLVR: So it's not unfree for you, making it, nor is it necessarily unfree for a truly great dancer, but there is a kind of strict structure that gets made.

ABP: Oh, more than a strict structure! Everything. The material itself. Of what your body is doing. Like if I said right now: *Oh, Jordan, don't actually use those fingers to pick up that card. I just want you to pick up that top card and put it on the table without using that hand, but that other hand: Can you put it behind your head, but extend your arm more slowly when you do that?* You'd go insane; it's terrible. You'd feel very unfree.

BLVR: Right, right.

ABP: But once you have it, once you have the experience, then it's like—within that, where am I? And it gets super interesting.

BLVR: You write in the book that at a certain point in history there arose a division

between the dancers and the watchers of the dance. And that gave rise to kinesthetic empathy, or the feeling we get when we watch someone leap through the air and *our* bodies also kind of leap inside. I wanted to ask how much you're playing with that space between the watcher and the dancer, the kinesthetic empathy that's between them. How much of that is also being choreographed?

ABP: I don't think you can choreograph it. I wish! I hear that and I'm like, Oh, what a fun question. Like, if you could only control how the audience's body experiences what you're doing. I can only say that I've had the experience when I've seen somebody jump very high. When I was a child I saw Baryshnikov leap—it was during his prime as a ballet dancer—and I saw him leap and I remember that his body was in the air for too long. Like it wasn't possible. He went up and he just hung out there, and I remember my body going [*big intake of breath*], and I felt the leap! And that's kinesthetic empathy. And I don't think you can choreograph that. I don't know how. I wish I could.

BLVR: You're very much in conversation with Merce Cunningham, but the quotation of his that leaped out the most to me when you quoted it in the book is "We give ourselves away at every moment."

ABP: Yeah, that's huge for me.

BLVR: It made me start thinking about your work as forensic, or anthropological—like, it made me wonder about the extent to which part of your practice is looking at the way we human beings in our pedestrian life are giving ourselves away, and then are trying to make art from that. Does it feel forensic to you at any point?

ABP: I'd say what you just described would describe certain roads I've gone down, yeah. I'm very interested in the pedestrian body in public space. There's no question about that. But some of it was reawakened through COVID because we were all choreographing out there and doing it *really well*. The citizen body was dancing perfectly. We were good at standing on our Xs, the whole thing. It was great. I was very impressed.

But of course this idea came from the Judsons, and when I was first learning choreography, that was the tradition. Anybody in downtown dance, of my generation, is going to be very affected by that. Speaking of Pina [Bausch], when I first saw her and I was, like, twenty-five, I put those two things together. Her theatricality, her interest in certain theatrical elements that the Judsons had completely thrown out—costume, personality, relationality. All those things. I combined those instantly without even thinking of it. The whole pedestrianism was essentially not enough for me, theatrically. I'm so interested in literature and plays and stuff.

BLVR: I know that when you've worked with David Byrne you've been interested in the way he naturally moves his body. How much is that a part of your process, in general—observing the way that the people who you're working with are moving in space?

ABP: I think it's more like observing what their strengths are, or what they lean into, as movers. David's such a natural dancer. My favorite quote from David was in some interview where somebody asked him about his early dances and he said, *Well, when I was making up my dances… I would just look in a mirror and try to do dances that nobody did. Like, try to make up movement that nobody did, that didn't look like anyone else's movement.* That's choreography to me. That's a choreographic mind.

BLVR: When did you notice the relationship between language and grammar and dance?

ABP: Poetry. I think I even say it in my book. With my mom, we'd memorize poems, my whole life, so I think intuitively I just felt the poetics in there. And then, as a person who, for want of a better word, is a formalist, I wasn't too long into my career before I brought those structures, those language structures, into choreography. Definitely straight from poetry.

BLVR: We'll end with my silliest question.

ABP: [*Laughs*] OK.

BLVR: What are your favorite verbs?

ABP: Not silly! I guess *to walk*, *to attach*, *to divine*. I actually have a series of verbs that I always go to when I'm making material.

BLVR: Do you have them written down somewhere?

ABP: Yeah, I mean in, like, all my notes, all these verbs. *To divine*, *to disassemble*, *to detach*, *to lay*.

BLVR: Maybe this question has the same answer, but I want to distinguish between what are your favorite verbs and what are the verbs of your practice. What are the verbs of your work?

ABP: That's a great question. *To craft. To construct. To shimmer.* I want to think of a word for "the surface." A verb. I can't quite think of it.

BLVR: Like *scrim*? I mean, that's a noun, but—

ABP: Like a verb for "the surface." Or the costume. The makeup. *To decorate*? [*Laughs*] To decorate. That was a totally fun question. I've never thought about that in my life. ✶

MICROINTERVIEW WITH NOOR NAGA, PART VII

THE BELIEVER: While reading the love story in *If an Egyptian Cannot Speak English*, I was reminded of the psychoanalytic concept of transference, wherein relationships are essentially just mutual or competing projections of individual fantasies. Janet Malcolm, for example, writes that "romantic love is fundamentally solitary." Does this resonate with you?

NOOR NAGA: In my personal life, in the real world, I would love to say no. But somehow, every time I write, that is very much the underlying acting principle that seems to come alive for my characters, which is sad. I don't know why I can't write real romance. I just write transference actually. Need to work on that. ✶

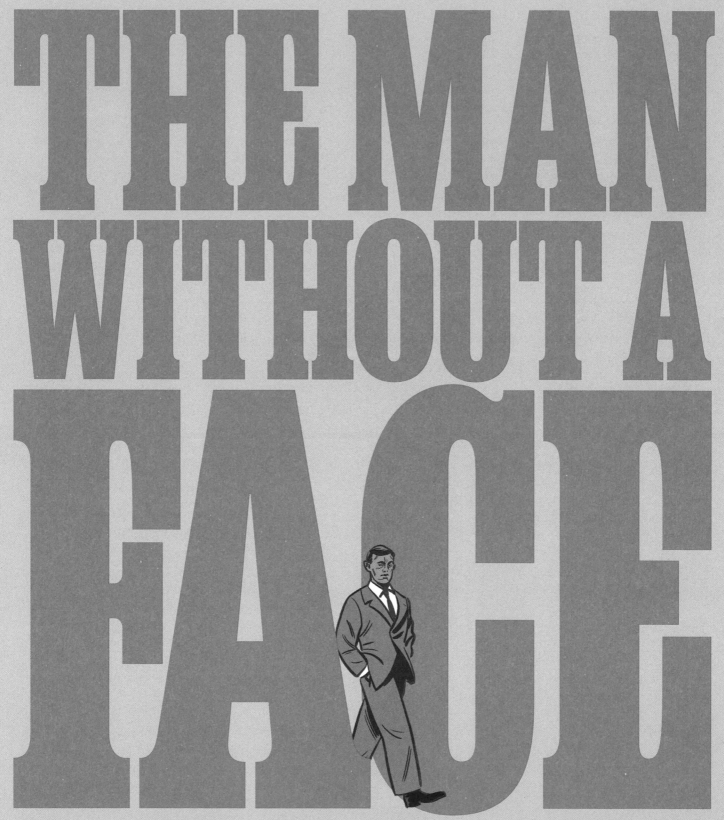

THE MAN WITHOUT A FACE

In search of the Asian actors who first played cinema's favorite Chinese American detective

by **KATIE GEE SALISBURY**

illustrations by **KRISTIAN HAMMERSTAD**

espite once being hailed as a role model, Charlie Chan hasn't held up well in the nearly one hundred years since his introduction. Many now see the "honorable Chinese detective" for what he is: a caricature plucked from the imagination of a white man. Earl Derr Biggers, to be precise, a Harvard graduate and former newspaperman who happened to stumble upon an interesting item in a Honolulu paper about a real-life Chinese detective named Chang Apana.

The only thing Charlie Chan has in common with the man who inspired him is his ability to reel in the bad guys. Chang Apana was a small, trim man, skilled with a bullwhip like an Asian Indiana Jones, steely-eyed in his pursuit of Honolulu's criminal element. He was a cowboy, a "paniolo," in the words of his biographer, Yunte Huang. Not the kind of guy who would be caught eating one too many jelly doughnuts.

Chan, by contrast, is a character only a novelist with a fanciful mind and little actual knowledge of Chinese people could invent. (The same goes for Sax Rohmer's supervillain, Fu Manchu.) Even among literature's many beloved detectives, Chan is unique. The affable sleuth first appeared in Biggers's *The House Without a Key*, which debuted as a serial novel in the January 24, 1925, issue of *The Saturday Evening Post*. But it wasn't until a quarter of the way into the novel that Charlie Chan made his grand entrance:

> He was very fat indeed, yet he walked with the light dainty step of a woman. His cheeks were as chubby as a baby's, his skin ivory tinted, his black hair close-cropped, his amber eyes slanting.

When a woman in desperate need of help learns he's the best detective in town and is the man assigned to her case, she sputters in protest, "But— he's Chinese!"

The thing about Charlie Chan is that in the films and television shows memorializing his adventures, he has *rarely* been Chinese, let alone Asian. "Favorite pastime of man is fooling himself," as the epigram-spouting Chan might say.

Swedish actor Warner Oland was the first to make Charlie Chan movie-star famous, in 1931's *Charlie Chan Carries On*. His yellowface depiction notwithstanding, Oland allegedly used almost no makeup to play the part. He simply combed his eyebrows up, turned the ends of his mustache down, and grew in a black goatee for good measure. Oland played Charlie Chan in sixteen films for Fox Film Corporation (later, 20th Century–Fox) and became synonymous with the detective in the 1930s—fans referred to him more often by Chan's name than his own. He fell into the habit of speaking in the same proverb-laced pidgin his character was best known for, even in the privacy of his own home. There was no escaping Chan, though that didn't stop Oland from trying. He nearly drank himself to death, then walked off the set of *Charlie Chan at the Ringside* one day in 1938 and sailed to his native Sweden, where he caught pneumonia and died.

Fox had no intention of letting its best-selling franchise die with Oland, and promptly replaced him with Sidney Toler, who went on to star in twenty-two films, followed by Roland Winters, who starred in six. Later, Charlie Chan was rebooted in a succession of films and television series, impersonated by actors J. Carrol Naish, Peter Ustinov, and Ross Martin. It was a plum job for a character actor of a certain vintage, a role one could age into. All that was required was a fatherly gravitas, some facial hair, and a middle-aged paunch to achieve that pleasantly plump silhouette in a white linen suit. You could be every kind of exotic white man, as the list of actors' names attests. Just leave it up to the makeup department to tape back your eyes and powder your face a few shades darker.

But what if Hollywood studios had cast an Asian actor in the role of Charlie Chan instead?

In fact, incredibly, they did. And it wasn't just one Asian actor, but three. Most historians gloss over the unremarkable films they appeared in, which make up the early Charlie Chan canon, because so little is known about them. It's a bittersweet irony that Charlie Chan has been defined by the white actors who played him in yellowface, yet he debuted in the hands of Asian actors—a detail that is mostly forgotten today. And so, turning this conundrum over in my head, I set out to solve a Charlie Chan mystery of my own.

Not long after *The House Without a Key*'s success, Pathé picked up the rights to produce it for the silent screen. As the American division of the French studio Pathé Frères, the company was best known for its early silent serials in the 1910s. Such tales perfected the cliffhanger format, like *The Perils of Pauline*, in which the title character is an independent young woman who insists on pursuing a few adventures before marrying her sweetheart. Unfolding over a dozen or more episodes, serials like this kept audiences guessing, wondering how

Promotional poster for Charlie Chan on Broadway, *the fifteenth Charlie Chan film starring Warner Oland. Produced by 20th Century–Fox, 1937; directed by Eugene Forde.*

the plucky heroine would get out of her latest fix.

Although movie serials had lost some of their shine by the mid-1920s, Pathé appears to have allocated plenty of resources to *The House Without a Key*. The ten-part feature was shot on location in Hawaii, and the studio cast top serial stars Allene Ray and Walter Miller. For the role of the Chinese

CLOCKWISE FROM TOP LEFT: New Mystery Adventures of Charlie Chan #6, 7, 8, 9; published by Charlton, 1955. The pencil work on issue 6 is credited to comic legend Jack Kirby.

more than a glorified extra, but he got to act alongside plenty of the silent era's stars, like Bebe Daniels, Fatty Arbuckle, and Jackie Coogan. Kuwa's headshot appeared regularly in the *Standard Casting Directory* and in the classifieds sections of *Camera!* and *Close Up*, where he advertised his talent for portraying Japanese and Chinese characters.

It makes sense that Kuwa, and not a white actor made up to look Asian, was the first to play Charlie Chan. Biggers did not originally intend for his Chinese detective to steal the show, and neither did Pathé—it billed Kuwa twelfth in the credits. Chan was a character who served a purpose. He was there to solve the mystery, unveil the villain, and then exit stage left. Director Spencer Gordon Bennet later admitted that *The House Without a Key* "was no Charlie Chan picture. Chan was just a detective. He wasn't that involved in the action."

If the film hadn't been lost, maybe we could decide for ourselves. Only a lingering still photograph holds a clue as to how Kuwa might have embodied Chan. In it, he wears a dark suit and a straw boater, his neatly cropped hair peeking out from beneath. The defiant killer is at the center of the scene, now in the clutches of his victim's family members, while Chan is merely a witness standing on the fringes.

The favorable reception of Biggers's follow-up, *The Chinese Parrot*, made it clear that the draw was Charlie Chan himself. Universal bought the rights to the novel in 1927 and tapped the newly arrived German import Paul Leni to direct a

detective, they brought on Japanese actor George Kuwa.

Born Keiichi Kuwahara to a respected judge in Hiroshima, Kuwa disappointed his father by ditching the family profession and setting his sights on Hollywood. He arrived in Los Angeles in the late 1910s and found work in the flickers playing bit roles in "Oriental" melodramas. He was a working actor, the kind whose parts were sometimes little silent adaptation. Leni was coming off his first Hollywood effort, the widely praised horror mystery *The Cat and the Canary*, and expectations were already high to see what he could do with a Charlie Chan mystery.

Universal cast well-known regulars to play the leads, including Marian Nixon and Hobart Bosworth. The Chinese American actor Anna May Wong (riding the fame from her role in Douglas Fairbanks's 1924 blockbuster *The Thief of Bagdad*) appeared as an exotic dancer who is swiftly murdered for the string of pearls around her ankle—the object at the center of the plot's many twists and turns. But who was to play Charlie Chan?

Kamiyama Sôjin, a Japanese actor with a storied career, was ultimately selected to try his hand at the role. (George Kuwa apparently wasn't considered for the role this time around and was instead demoted to background work.) Sôjin, as he was commonly known, had been a leader in Japan's modern theater movement, producing and acting in productions of Shakespeare, Ibsen, Sudermann, and Shaw. When he and his actress wife, Yamakawa Uraji, arrived in Hollywood on their first trip to America in 1919, they were hailed as "the Sothern and Marlowe of Japan," a reference to a famous Shakespearean acting duo.

Such lofty comparisons did much to extend Sôjin's reputation throughout Hollywood. Once he returned in 1923 and was cast in *The Thief of Bagdad*, his screen presence became self-evident. Critics took notice of his masterful turn as the evil Mongol prince, and he soon gained a reputation for wicked expressions and brooding looks.

According to Sôjin, though, he wasn't the first in line to play Charlie Chan in *The Chinese Parrot*. In his memoir, *Sugao no Hariuddo* (Hollywood without makeup), Sôjin explains that it was actually Conrad Veidt, one of Leni's longtime collaborators and a fellow German, who was initially cast as Chan. Yet no matter how they did his makeup, Veidt simply didn't look Chinese.

Sôjin was called in to assist. He was so successful at transforming Veidt's appearance that Universal wanted to hire him to do Veidt's makeup for the entirety of the film. Sôjin refused outright. "I told them I was not a makeup man and left," he recalled. Outplayed, Universal threw up its hands, fired Veidt, and installed Sôjin in his place. Veidt was so shattered, Sôjin later claimed, that he sat in his dressing room and cried. "I felt sorry for Conrad Veidt, so I found a great script called *The Man Who Laughs* for him," Sôjin added somewhat sardonically, putting his own spin on the sequence of events. Veidt did later star in *The Man Who Laughs*, Paul Leni's next film, but it's doubtful that Sôjin was the one to suggest the Victor Hugo novel from which the script was adapted.

The Chinese Parrot opened in the fall of 1927 to mixed reviews. Some critics felt the film's plot was rather thin, leaving little to be surprised about at its resolution. Others, however, were spellbound by the vivid, creepy atmosphere that Leni evoked through his off-kilter set design, wonky angles, and use of camera techniques like double exposure—core features of German expressionism.

Above all, Sôjin's commanding performance, not only as Charlie Chan but also in a series of disguises, seemed to make up for whatever the story lacked.

"The character acting of the Japanese screen player… is perhaps the most interesting of any in the picture," one reviewer wrote. "True, Sôjin was in his element in such an Oriental role," another critic observed, "but that doesn't detract from the remarkable 'scoop' he pulled in putting the breathing life into this picture." A columnist for the British magazine *The Sketch* remarked, "[Sôjin] juggles his face and body in the most amazing way… His least gesture has intention; his moments of stillness are pregnant with meaning. And, to cap it all, he has a great sense of humour."

It's no shock that Sôjin, one of Japan's preeminent actors, was a marvel as Charlie Chan, bringing his own distinct interpretation to the role. Alas, two months after the film's premiere, a studio fire destroyed Universal's print of *The Chinese Parrot*, most likely the master copy. No other print is known to exist.

A cache of film stills on IMDb offers a small consolation and a chance to search for traces of Sôjin's performance. In some of the scenes pictured, he's disguised in "coolie" garb. He stoops over comically, to almost half his height, with an obsequious expression, as he serves various distinguished houseguests from a silver platter. Returned to his upright form as the honorable detective, he has a strikingly different bearing, exuding confidence and cunning. In every frame in which he appears, all eyes are fixed in his direction.

"Our gaunt corpse-like Chinese [*sic*] actor friend So-Jin, with his parchment skin and prawnish movements, retains your almost undivided attention during the time he is seen," *Picturegoer* remarked, "and he is seen quite a lot." I'll hazard to suggest that Sôjin could have had a notable career ahead of him as Charlie Chan. But that future was not to be.

Earl Derr Biggers was optimistic about cinema's ability to enshrine his hero in pop culture "as the leading sleuth of his generation." And though he didn't have much involvement in the film adaptations of his novels, he did have control over whom he sold the rights to. Biggers admired Sôjin's prowess as an actor, but, as he wrote in a private letter to his editor, Sôjin gave the appearance of "a long, thin, sinister chink." He was nothing like the charmingly chubby Charlie Chan that Biggers had dreamed up in his novels. Months later, after being informed by friends and family who had gone to see the finished film and pronounced it "terrible beyond belief," Biggers lamented, "The general opinion of people out here is that I ought to sue Universal for defamation of character."

Best-selling author or not, Biggers bought into stereotypes about the Chinese as much as anyone else. In the white racist imagination, a "bad Chinese" was a stealthy schemer who couldn't be trusted. But not his Chan. By contrast, his creation was a fountain of benign wisdom, there to help the white man in his hour of need. Chan was nonthreatening, childlike in his corpulence. Biggers credited himself with inventing this characterization:

Promotional poster for Charlie Chan in Panama, *an unauthorized adaptation of the novel* Marie Galante. *Produced by 20th Century–Fox, 1940; directed by Norman Foster.*

"Sinister and wicked Chinese are old stuff, but an amiable Chinese on the side of law and order had never been used." Some today would call his vision of a "good Chinese" by another name: the model minority.

For the next book in the series, *Behind That Curtain*, the film rights went to neither Pathé nor Universal, but to Fox Film Corporation. It was also to be the first Charlie Chan flick produced with sound. Thus, even if Fox had thought to cast Sôjin, his halting, accented English made him an unfavorable candidate.

Here's where the plot thickens. Fox recruited a man named E. L. Park to play Charlie Chan. Though I had long known about Kuwa's and Sôjin's stints as the Chinese detective, I hadn't heard of Park until I received an email from a friend last year, containing a screenshot from an obscure blog with a photo of the actor. Based on his surname, the blogger guessed he must be Korean. More mysterious still, *Behind That Curtain* was Park's sole film credit, yet he hardly appeared in it. He was dropped in at the movie's end, deus ex machina–style, for two minutes of screen time, as the case appears to solve itself. Charlie Chan was but an accessory to one of Scotland Yard's global crime investigations.

So who exactly was E. L. Park? My search took me to one of the twenty-first century's most popular sleuthing portals: ancestry.com. (Luckily, this amateur detective already had a subscription.) Soon I was staring at a complete family tree for Edward Leon Park and his relatives. What's more, Ed Park, as he was more often called, was not the only person in his family to make his way into showbiz. His wife, Florence Park, known by the stage name Oie Chan, and his daughters, Bo-Ling and Bo-Ching, who branded themselves as the "Chinese twins" for their vaudeville routine, were regular bit players in Hollywood.

Several messages and email chains later, I was connected with Bo-Gay Tong Salvador, Ed Park's

Promotional still from Charlie Chan Carries On. *This 1931 film marked the first appearance of Warner Oland as Charlie Chan. While this film is considered lost, Fox simultaneously filmed a Spanish-language version, released under the title* Eran trece, *and directed by Hamilton MacFadden— and this version has survived.*

granddaughter, who is now in her seventies and working to capture her family's fascinating history. Bo-Gay greeted me over Zoom from her home in Southern California and told me about her grandfather.

The first mystery she cleared up was that of his ethnicity. Park, she explained, was neither Korean nor white, as some people wrongly assumed when looking at his name on paper. He was a second-generation Chinese American born in San Francisco's Chinatown in 1881, and his Chinese name was Leong Gwai June. At the time, most Americans were unfamiliar with the conventions of Chinese names, which are sequenced with the family name before one's given name. His older brother's Chinese name was transliterated into English as Leon

Quai Park. Since "Park" was assumed to be his surname, he went by Robert Park. Whether the name was applied to Edward by association or he chose it because he saw the advantages of an Americanized name, Leong Gwai June became known as Edward Leon Park. Leon was a nod to his true family name.

I asked Bo-Gay what led to her grandfather's foray into Hollywood. Her answer meandered, much like the journey she described. Ed Park was a jack-of-all-trades who did whatever he could to support his family. As a young man, he enlisted in the US Navy, and later served as a cook on the USS *Albatross* as it charted the waters from San Francisco to Japan on an oceanographic expedition. When he returned to the mainland, he settled

THE SPACE WHERE I MAKE A LIFE IS A RENTED ROOM

by Cathy Linh Che

I retrofitted a shelter.
Burned driftwood.
Drove a gash across the country,

slept in the car, dreaming,
of you. I was in love
and erasing the gap.

I drew a line
and watched
it shake.

Dark rose
of the afternoon,
spillway into the delta,

I wept, blistering. Pinned
photos to a clothesline—
and leapt into each one.

---

down in Berkeley, California, and married Florence Chan, his sister-in-law's best friend, who had grown up in a Protestant mission home.

In 1910, he was hired as one of the first Chinese interpreters at the newly established Angel Island Immigration Station (the West Coast counterpart to Ellis Island, for processing new arrivals from across the Pacific). Despite his full-time government job, the always-resourceful Park found ways to make a little extra on the side. He ran a produce cart business, bought a farm that raised chickens and pigeons, and helped out at the *Chinese World* newspaper, where his brother was the managing editor. Park proved his adaptability through his wide-ranging portfolio, and the skills he picked up along the way served him well in his future endeavors. I can imagine a young Charlie Chan soaking up a similar hodgepodge of experiences, background work for his final act as police detective.

By 1927, Park moved with his wife and two daughters, now sixteen and nineteen, to Los Angeles, where he got a job as an interpreter for the city courts and immigration offices. The move was likely influenced by Bo-Ling and Bo-Ching's desire to break into the movies. The girls were a talented singing and dancing duo and had been performing on the vaudeville circuit since they were preteens. Park also spied a business opportunity. After nearly two decades of experimentation, Hollywood was finally coming into its own.

In addition to his interpreter job, Park opened a Chinese restaurant and the China Costume Company on Alameda Street in downtown Los Angeles. The costume store supplied various studios with authentic-looking garments for their "Oriental" features, which were strangely in demand. One day Irving Cummings, the director of *Behind That Curtain*, walked into the store and, sizing up Park, decided he'd found his Charlie Chan. Indeed, with his broad oblong face, slightly balding head, and stout figure, Park looked the part. Years later, a newspaper reporter who chanced to meet him recalled being immediately "struck by his uncanny resemblance to Biggers' fictional Chan."

Though his cameo in *Behind That Curtain* amounts to a precious few minutes, Park leaves a memorable impression. He looks dignified sitting at his desk in a three-piece suit and speaks his lines matter-of-factly. While his English lacks polish, it's infinitely easier to listen to than that of the Scotland Yard inspector, with his drawn-out pronunciation. Park appears most at ease when he gets up mid-conversation to address the racket coming from the building next door. He scolds a young saxophone player in fluent Cantonese, flashes a mischievous smile at the boy's acquiescence, and then returns to his desk.

Park never acted again, but his one flirtation with Hollywood secured his place in moviemaking history as the first Chinese American to play Charlie Chan. His wife and daughters continued to appear sporadically in films over the years, including in roles as the wife and daughters to—who else?—Charlie Chan. I asked Bo-Gay what she thought of this family legacy (as a three-year-old, she herself appeared in the 1954 film *World for Ransom*). "While I am proud because they were proud of their accomplishments, I do have mixed feelings," she said. "I know that many of their roles were relegated to the stereotypes given to Asians."

Edward Leon Park might not have been an actor or a detective, but in many ways, he's the Charlie Chan we deserve. Like the fictional Chan, he was a man caught in the crosscurrents of two societies. He was a "culture broker," as historian Mae Ngai has termed such cultural go-betweens, navigating the worlds of both his community and white American society, always seeking ways to bridge the two. And like Chan, he was a family man who raised his children to join the next generation of Americans building this country. Maybe Ed Park, though overlooked, was Charlie Chan's truest incarnation.

As Chan himself would say, "Door of opportunity swing both ways." In this case, the door swung irrevocably shut. Following Park's appearance, the appetite for casting another Asian actor to play Charlie Chan fizzled out. Biggers, in fact, was ready to give up completely: "The news is all about over there that Charlie cannot be cast—Fox tried every Chinese

Promotional poster for The Chinese Cat *(a.k.a.* Murder in the Funhouse*), a mystery film starring Sidney Toler as Charlie Chan. The film (originally titled* Charlie Chan and the Perfect Crime*) was the second Charlie Chan movie from Monogram Pictures, and was released in 1944.*

laundryman on the Coast, but never thought of trying an actor—and the issue looks like a dead one."

Then Warner Oland came along. He put on the white linen suit, something Chang Apana never wore, and it fit. Just as Biggers had rewritten Chang to match his conception of a Honolulu police detective, Oland recast Charlie Chan in his own image. Chan, at heart, was merely a white man posing in a Chinese detective's clothing. ★

PLACE

LAC DU BOIS, BEMIDJI, MINNESOTA

by Ruby Sutton

FEATURES:
- ✯ Miniature Eiffel Tower
- ✯ Children of tiger parents
- ✯ Twelve miles from the Paul Bunyan and Babe the Blue Ox statue

They said "Bonjour" and looked at me with their eyes wide, and already I felt slightly frightened, unsure if my tongue could produce the sounds they were searching for. I'd spent the last two hours gazing out at the pine trees while my mother and I listened to language tapes in preparation, until she finally turned right onto Road Thorsenvein. I felt a tingle of nervous anticipation as we passed a group of children kicking a ball around in the Fußballplatz, then a diamantine sign that read FUTURE WORLD LEADERS AT WORK AND AT PLAY. My mother followed the signs for Lac du Bois and told me to get out at the parking lot.

When my parents first suggested I go to a language-immersion camp, I got excited about learning Chinese, imagining I might come out as a CIA recruit by the end of the summer. But because of my parents' Francophilia—and a vague family tradition of running around Paris intoxicated—I ended up at French camp instead. Now at the entrance gate, I could see a replica of the Eiffel Tower, only six feet tall, and in the distance a giant chessboard: the pawns were my height and the queen had fallen.

The counselors were asking what I wanted my new name to be. I'd thought on the drive that I might want to be Madeline or Amelie, but when I looked at the list of pseudonyms on their clipboard, those names were already taken. Instead, I proposed Gigi, not yet cognizant that it evoked the whimsical sensuality of a burlesque dancer.

The counselors wrote the name on a wooden plaque, attached it to a piece of string, and hung it around my neck. My mother kissed me on both cheeks and disappeared into our Volkswagen. I was guided into a building called Paris, where rows of other children sat with identical tags hanging around their necks, fellow participants in the "Grand Simulation."

Concordia Language Villages (CLV) was founded in 1961, the vision of Gerhard Haukebo, a professor at Concordia College in Moorhead, Minnesota. Although he was raised in the small town of Roseau, Haukebo had always nursed visions of connecting the globe: as a child, he envisioned building a tunnel to China from the backyard of his parents farm, although his dreams didn't stop there. After college, he spent four years working as a teacher and principal at a German military base, instructing American children, where he was impressed by how much his students absorbed through play outside the classroom. After joining the faculty at Concordia in 1959, Haukebo proposed that the college sponsor an innovative language-immersion program that would teach students how to apply language in everyday life rather than focusing on grammar. In 1961, Concordia rented out the Luther Crest Bible camp in nearby Alexandria, and seventy-two campers, ages nine through twelve, participated in Haukebo's two-week immersive German-language experiment, called Waldsee, that summer.

Today there are fifteen CLV camps, all built with "authentic architecture," located on an eight-hundred-acre lakeshore property in Bemidji, Minnesota, that CLV purchased from a woolen-apparel manufacturer. At Salolampi, campers are invited to take Finnish-style saunas daily. Sjölunden is modeled after a Swedish fishing village, complete with a weaving studio. Sup sogŭi Hosu, built on what used to be a resort, was recently endowed with a generous scholarship program that sends Koreans out to Bemidji, so campers can learn from these native speakers.

Styled like a Bavarian village and boasting alumni like Chelsea Clinton, Waldsee is the biggest of the camps. When I visited Waldsee as a kid with the other Lac du Bois campers for a game of flag football, I heard a rumor that the German government had funded the program to improve their postwar reputation. In 2018, the camp was embarrassed to discover that *Waldsee* was a euphemism for "Auschwitz," when one curious parent typed "Waldsee" and "Nazi" into his search bar.

Illustration by Pete Gamlen

At $2,600 for two weeks, the tuition is prohibitive for many Bemidji families, but CLV's assistant director of alumni relations and giving, Ross Dybvig, tells me that the camps, and the influx of tourism they bring, are well received by the community. For example, Dybvig told me that the people of Bemidji often encounter CLV campers wearing name tags while shopping at Target with their families. "They see our kids buying things," he said. "It's always a good experience."

A COMPILATION OF LAST WORDS FROM HOLLYWOOD'S MOST KILLED-OFF ACTOR, SEAN BEAN

* *Caravaggio* (1986): "For you… For *us*."
* *War Requiem* (1989): "[No spoken dialogue in movie]"
* *The Field* (1990): "Stop, Da! Nobody betrayed you!"
* *Clarissa* (1991): "Clarissa, let this redeem my sins."
* *Patriot Games* (1992): "That's not my mission!"
* *GoldenEye* (1995): "For England, James?"
* *Airborne* (1998): "It's all done with, Bill. Mr. Melo is—"
* *The Fellowship of the Ring* (2001): "I would have followed you, my brother. My captain. My king."
* *Equilibrium* (2002): "A heavy cost. I pay it gladly."
* *Henry VIII* (2003): "God bless the one Catholic Church of England."
* *The Island* (2005): "I brought you into this world… and I can take you out of it."
* *Far North* (2007): "Oh, God. God, no! No! No! No! No! No! No! No! No!"
* *Outlaw* (2007): "'Rubbish,' he says. Eh? Rubbish! You know, Monroe? You know something? I've never heard you swear. Takes a lot of doing for a man in your shoes."
* *The Hitcher* (2007): "Feels good, doesn't it?"
* *Red Riding: The Year of Our Lord 1974* (2009): "Fuckin' hell, I'm no angel."
* *Ca$h* (2010): "I'll fucking kill you both!"
* *Game of Thrones* (2011): "Joffrey Baratheon is the one true heir to the Iron Throne, by the grace of all the gods, lord of the Seven Kingdoms, and protector of the realm."
* *Age of Heroes* (2011): "You go, I'll cover you!"

—list compiled by Bryce Woodcock

My first summer at Lac du Bois, I learned of faraway places like Monterey Bay and Westchester. When I visited New York on a family vacation the following year, I got to go to the Harvard Club with my new friend Bruno, who took the train down from the suburbs with his mother. As if testing me, his mother asked if I laughed at the cartoons in *The New Yorker*. After my first Lac du Bois summer, I returned to middle school in the small Minnesota town where I grew up, slightly unsure of how to talk about my French camp experience with my best friend, Kayla, who'd spent the summer dodging the BB-gun shots of her older brothers.

They say that when you speak another language, you become another person. Perhaps this is why one summer I decided to flush my bottle of fluoxetine down the toilet in the Paris building. This was after breakfast, when the camp awarded "Super Français" beads to the dedicated campers who had gone the past twenty-four hours without speaking English. Being under constant surveillance, it was all I could do to take charge of my situation. Or maybe I decided that Gigi was too cheerful a name for someone who needed their serotonin artificially regulated. I started crying during rest time, when I received letters from my parents. For the rest of camp, Benoît, the counselor stationed at the Village First Aid, monitored my treatment, finding me each day at breakfast with a little blue pill in his hands and watching me swallow it.

After this, Lac du Bois was bliss. I made friends. There were choreographed dances. I had my first kiss—or maybe it was one of the other campers, Amelie or Madeline. The memories are fuzzy now, but for someone, behind the Paris building, it happened. I developed a crush on my favorite counselor, Cheikh, who claimed to be a Senegalese prince. I imagined going to Dakar and mingling with the royal family, but it turned out he was dating another counselor, Caroline, who slept in the bunk bed below mine. It didn't matter. I learned to love them both equally, as if they were my parents. I went back the next summer, and the one after that, and though I kept asking my parents to send me to learn Chinese, they insisted I finish what I'd started and go back to French camp. Now, I occasionally find myself with half-completed applications for the Middlebury Language Schools when I'm up late at night with insomnia. I still know the lyrics to "Elle me dit" by heart, and sometimes, in the back of my head, I hear it. ✶

NATHANIEL DORSKY

[FILMMAKER]

"EXPERIMENTAL FILMS ARE A LITTLE BIT LIKE WEEDS—SEEDS THAT
GOT CAUGHT BETWEEN THE CRACKS IN THE SIDEWALK."

Why Anthology Film Archives in New York City is
Nathaniel Dorsky's favorite place to screen a film:
It has perfect sight lines
The crowd is great
It has an Eastman projector
The projector was built by a man named James Bond

No filmmaker more joyfully and succinctly embodies the poetry of the *medium than Nathaniel Dorsky. A recipient of a Guggenheim Fellowship and grants from the Rockefeller Foundation and the National Endowment for the Arts, Dorsky has been making experimental films since 1963. His films are silent and use the intimacy of that silence to draw us deeper into the subtle beauty of his images. Luminous combinations of shapes and light fill the screen, revealing the mysteries of our everyday life and offering glimpses of the sublime. His films are shot and screened exclusively on 16 mm, so screenings are rare events. Few have been as lucky as I was when, on an afternoon in January 2023, after a bite of exquisite dark chocolate, I was led through a trapdoor in his living room, down a set of stairs into the darkly glowing sanctuary where he edits his films, and treated to a private screening of two new works:* Dialogues *and* Place d'or, *the latter of which he had finished tweaking just the night before. As the projector began to roll*

Illustration by Kristian Hammerstad

and Dorsky's images filled the wall at eighteen frames per second, the medicinal quality of his work immediately took hold.

In Dialogues, *the first film he screened, flowers, branches, and other similar forms shimmered with a vibrant fragility, becoming sculptural beings that communed with one another within the frames. About halfway through the piece, the projection darkened completely, until I noticed a milky-white swirl in the upper-left-hand corner. Suddenly, the whole screen brightened and a clear image of the Pacific Ocean emerged: the milky-white swirl became a foggy summer sky balanced above equally murky water. Shot at a diagonal, a solitary oil tanker could then be seen moving across the horizon, slowly making its way toward the bay. The clarity of this image, its devastating grays juxtaposed with the abstraction of the previous cut, thrust me into a bardo-like confusion. It felt akin to what the first viewers of* North by Northwest *must have felt when the crop duster swoops down from the sky and begins flying directly toward an unsuspecting Cary Grant. The image stayed with me until days later, when, in a dream, I found myself on a beach, a giant whale's tail rising from the water, threatening to crash down on me and my umbrella through the foggy sky.*

The pretense for my being in San Francisco and spending the afternoon with Dorsky was a performance at Gray Area on Mission Street, part of a short tour I was doing promoting my album Wendy *that was soon to be released on Fat Possum Records. My San Francisco show comprised two parts: the first, a live improvised score to films by two other luminary filmmakers, Harry Smith and Jordan Belson, performed by me, Ben Goldberg, Michael Coleman, and Jordan Glenn; and the second, a set of songs from my record. It might seem incongruous for a musician, especially one who often works with film in both composed and improvised contexts, to be captivated by a silent filmmaker, but I can't help but feel that Dorsky's films are singing to me. As he said in our conversation, "They're not films without sound; they're silent films. Which means the silence has to be palpable."*

The following interview took place at Dorsky's home. In his cozy and vibrant apartment, built during World War II for shipbuilders and their families, I studied the curious colored glass electrical insulators that lined the windows, as well as several reproductions of works by the early Renaissance Italian painter Piero della Francesca that adorned the walls. We sat in his living room as our conversation swooped and swerved through an array of fascinating and unexpected topics. While we spoke, the green, gold, blue, pink, and purple auras created from light passing through the insulators glowed.

—*Will Epstein*

I. NOT QUITE FLOWERS

THE BELIEVER: When I first walked in we began talking about these cutouts of Piero della Francesca paintings you have around your apartment. Do you think a lot about painting when you're shooting, or is that a different mindset?

NATHANIEL DORSKY: Oh, yes, very much. Painting seems closer to film than photography. Still photography is an instant and you expand out from that one moment, but film takes place in time in the same way as painting does— a good painting might have twenty minutes that it gives you. Also, I try not to use film as a type of journalism or as a window into something, but rather to turn the screen itself into something.

BLVR: You turn the screen into a world.

ND: Yeah, into a world.

BLVR: I know it's very touristy of me, but whenever I'm in San Francisco I can't help but think about *Vertigo* and Hitchcock. I think a lot of those filmmakers who came from the silent era talk about wanting to create a language that's unique to film in a way that feels somewhat similar to what you're talking about.

ND: *Vertigo* is a very powerful urban poem for this city. Hitchcock's brilliance is that the stories are a montage. In other words, his films are not a story that he photographs. The story itself is the nature of shots and cuts. People always say, *Oh, this film is Hitchcockian*, but it is rarely true.

BLVR: Yeah, when people say that, they're talking about something that just has to do with plot points. People also consider him the filmmaker who is super into psychology and symbolism, but that in a way feels kind of surface-level to what's actually going on.

ND: There are a lot things you are told are true that aren't true.

BLVR: That is true. [*Laughs*]

ND: You know the [Jean] Renoir film *Rules of the Game*?

BLVR: Yes.

ND: When I was growing up, the critics were basically leftists and all the leftist critics were saying, *It's a takedown of the upper class.* So you go to the movie and you say to yourself, Hm, I guess it's a takedown of the upper class. Then one time you'll see it without that at all and you'll realize it's fabulous. It's just fabulous and you can really experience the love of it all. I mean, probably my favorite films are narrative fiction. Experimental films are a little bit like weeds—seeds that got caught between the cracks in the sidewalk. We're not quite flowers, but then again, wildflowers are the most tender.

II. THE RINGS OF SATURN

BLVR: I think the first time I saw your films was at Anthology Film Archives for *The Arboretum Cycle*.

ND: Oh, you were there? That's my favorite place. It has perfect sight lines. It has the best projector, which is called the Eastman 25 or Eastman 40, which was built by a man named James Bond. He's the go-to person in America for projectors. And the crowd is great.

BLVR: Yes, very devoted.

ND: It's just fun. It's one of the few places that would make me want to get on a plane. I've been writing them, calling, and leaving messages, because I have these new films I want to show. You know, *The Arboretum Cycle* was sort of a turning point; it started a different arc—one based less on the various and more on deepening the specifics of one thing. All the films I've done since are a special group of films. A lot of them are shorter—some of them seven minutes, nine minutes, you know—but it seems they do everything they have to do in that amount of time. There's no need for them to be longer. They accomplish what has to be accomplished. I don't want it to be like when someone you know starts to talk a little too long about the same thing.

BLVR: As somebody who works in sound and music, I also felt like the sound of silence in that room was such a moving

thing. It was very powerful, almost like there was a sound emitting out from the screen.

ND: Definitely. In other words, they're not films without sound; they're silent films. Which means the silence has to be palpable.

BLVR: And it has a shape to it that changes as the film goes along too.

ND: Yeah, you're really working with the shape. I guess it's more like dance that way. Like tension and release—that kind of thing.

BLVR: Do you think at all about the sound in the room while the film is screening?

ND: No, like Cage? Do you know that piece by John Cage?

BLVR: Yes, "4'33"." It premiered in Woodstock, New York actually.

ND: Oh, yeah, I know that story. I've worked on many documentaries and it always comes up.

BLVR: In almost every documentary.

ND: Find me one that doesn't mention it. [*Laughs*]

BLVR: I just did the score for this documentary about Nam June Paik. I think they tell that story.

ND: It's like, *Hold on, here it comes!* Of course, it's always different because of the four minutes. [*His phone pings.*] It must be the dentist. [*Reading the text aloud*] "Yes, I am at my dentist." Oh, now Jerome, my partner, is at the dentist.

BLVR: Do you guys go to the same dentist?

ND: Yes.

BLVR: Maybe I should go. I don't like my dentist that much.

ND: Do you like nitrous?

Four stills from The Arboretum Cycle. *Images courtesy of Peter Blum Gallery.*

BLVR: I feel like I haven't had enough to know.

ND: That's the spirit. If you have the nerve, ask for nitrous just for a cleaning. It's kind of interesting. It's like you go out to where you're sitting on one of the rings of Saturn, looking up at the nighttime sky, and then you hear this voice that says, "Open a little," and you go right back to the chair and you move your head to the right. You do what you're supposed to do. It isn't like you're out of control, but it makes the pain very enjoyable. They could charge you anything for that and you'd do it.

BLVR: Sounds amazing.

ND: The dental chairs are located in a greenhouse in the backyard with tropical plants and music.

BLVR: Wait, this sounds way, way better than my dentist in all ways.

ND: Anyway, the nitrous is interesting. You know what's really good is if you're getting a root canal or a post, or something that's gonna take an hour and a half or two hours, then it's timeless on the nitrous. You have no idea how long you've been there. There's no time. Anyway, I know it's a little childish to speak about the dentist in this way.

BLVR: [*Laughs*] No, it's great. But back to what we were saying about your films. They feel very much like music to me.

ND: Well, Jerome, my partner, and I are big fans of, I guess what you call in the Western tradition "classical music," but also all kinds of world music and stuff.

BLVR: Yeah, there's something in a Mozart symphony where you feel that the placement of every note is done with intention and that's very much how I feel watching your movies—like each gesture of light or each cut has some alchemical purpose to it.

ND: Well, one thing I was gonna say is, I don't believe young people like classical music. There's a very good conservatory here in San Francisco called the San Francisco Conservatory of Music, and they have two or three concerts a week that are free, and it's so wonderful because the audience is filled with music students. We have such a good time. Besides that crowd, though, I don't sense that young people are in touch with classical music.

BLVR: It doesn't seem like it.

ND: They only know music as an adornment to language.

BLVR: Or as an adornment to life something that's just there in the background and taken for granted.

ND: There's that, but what I mean is, they don't know about music itself being the emotional landscape of a human being. They don't know that. And so it limits their film-making tremendously. Because if your film or your music comes out of itself, each moment develops into the next moment. It's very different if you're directing it from outside the piece. It never deepens if the film isn't going forward out of its own newness.

BLVR: Watching your work, I feel like I'm seeing both

improvisation and composition at work. Do you think in those terms at all?

ND: Yes, because—if I may call it [this]—"the creation" is a combination of chance followed by judgment, and judgment in "the creation" is reality. If something works, if it functions, it survives, and if it doesn't, it dies. But the initial thing at work is chance. How many planets do you have to throw onto the table before one works, so to speak, from our point of view? You might have to throw a few hundred. But then the one that works, works. So in that sense we're sort of talking about a combination of chance and discretion. I mean, it's interesting to call a certain period of four minutes of sound "the work," like Cage does, and it's different every time you perform it, but in a certain way, it's declaring *nothing* to be *something*.

BLVR: That's a lot of the work of making something, though.

ND: Someone might say, *What's the difference between openness and discretion? How can you be open and discreet?* Well, the openness involves being open to what you experience. In other words, you have an idea, you're gonna take a chance and put it down—then the important thing is to be open to your reaction to it. And that's where discretion comes in, by being open to your reaction. That means you don't let Mr. Lazy convince you that everything in your film is working perfectly. For instance, maybe you're working on a film and every time it comes to a certain shot, you realize you're spaced-out. Every time. And finally you go, Why am I always spaced out during this shot? Or: Why is my mind telling me it's good? Which, of course, means it's bad.

BLVR: So you listen to yourself in those moments and that's where the discretion comes.

ND: Yeah, and finally Mr. Lazy goes, *Oh! It's because the shot before is two seconds too long, and because it's too long, you're done by the time you come to the cut*. Things like that. But the main thing is to be open to your own reaction. Especially [as I'm] getting older, I realize it doesn't involve memory. It just involves recollecting your experience when you first saw the shot. What did I actually feel when that happened?

And I find I can remember that because it's sort of a body–muscle memory kind of thing. You can remember when that shot came on, and no matter what your brain rationalized, it wasn't right, even though you wanted it to be, because you're ready to move on.

BLVR: It's a very nourishing feeling to be in touch with yourself in that way.

ND: Yeah, it's fun and then it becomes a real practice, the art-making. It's the practice of being self-observant. You don't have to be observant of the thing you're making: that happens automatically. The honest part of your mind delivers the answers a couple of seconds before the narrator does. At least that's my experience. A lot of times, I'm doing things and I know the answer but Mr. Mind has to go and think about it first and then state to me the answer. But as I'm doing that, I'm going to myself, Wait a minute. I already know the answer. I already know it. You're busy saying this to yourself but you already know it. You already had the experience.

BLVR: I really feel that kind of openness, too, when I'm watching your films, and I think there's a kind of buoyancy that comes with that. I don't think *humor* is the right word, exactly, but I think there's a lightness and a buoyancy that are very enlivening.

ND: *Refreshing*, maybe, is a good word.

BLVR: *Refreshing*, yes. Do you feel like that kind of openness translates to when you're shooting? Even in regard to the technical process of shooting, do you have a filmic language that you've developed and are working with, or do you try to start from zero every time?

ND: Well, through your lifetime, everything changes. There was a long period of time, maybe twenty years, when I was making these polyvalent pieces, where every shot moved forward for its own reason and reverberated with other shots

you'd seen in the film. Then at a certain point, I got tired of the problem-solving of that. I'd start a film and go, Oh, I don't want these things. I know these problems. So then I asked myself, What would be new for me? What would be real for me? And then, ironically, I went to an earlier stage, back to when I was about nineteen or twenty. Moving forward was like coming back. It started during *The Arboretum Cycle* with a lot of articulation happening just through the film getting brighter and darker. Now I'm in this phase where I've made about twenty films like that and I drive people mad [*laughs*], getting brighter and darker. But it was a way of treating the Bolex more like an instrument than as a recording device. So I'll be out shooting and looking at something and the breeze comes and I open the lens so the frame starts to fill with light and then I darken it down. It's very similar to playing a musical instrument, I think, and you can start to play yourself as an instrument, in a sense.

BLVR: Right, it becomes an extension of yourself. It's interesting that *The Arboretum Cycle* films are the first films I saw of yours, because they really felt so fresh to me. So it makes sense hearing that you were just coming to something new.

ND: I had the theory for a long time, but I didn't have the courage to enact it. Well, I don't know if it's courage, but it took a while.

BLVR: It's just a natural process, maybe, of digesting.

ND: It first happened with a film in which I took things from all these failed projects and made something else altogether from the material.

BLVR: That's a good feeling.

III. CROWN JEWELS OF THE WIRE

ND: Do you know what an insulator is?

BLVR: Like the things on top of power lines?

ND: On top of telephone poles.

BLVR: Do they still make them? I've never seen anything like these before. [*Points to the window*]

ND: No, these are from the age of the opaque ceramic insulator.

BLVR: But these are glass, right?

ND: Yes, and I have ceramic ones too. I started to collect them when I was a kid and so have amassed these over many, many years. Collectors got excited about insulators because they were usually made by bottle companies who produced them without any intent for the color. They just used scraps of glass but they came out in all these fantastic variations.

BLVR: Kind of like sea glass.

ND: Oh, do you want to see my sea glass collection?

BLVR: Oh my god, I would love to.

ND: Not everyone gets to see this…

MICROINTERVIEW WITH NOOR NAGA, PART VIII

THE BELIEVER: Part of *If an Egyptian Cannot Speak English* is footnoted with both accurate and inaccurate details, playing with the formalities of academic texts as well as the expectations of the Western gaze. It made me wonder about your own interest in footnotes. Are you a staunch footnote reader?

NOOR NAGA: Yes, I like paratextual trivia. I like footnotes. I like acknowledgments pages. Any kind of marginalia if it's a used book. But I don't do any research on the writers I'm reading. I don't really want to know where they've lived or who they are. I want the stuff that's *in* the book but slightly off-center or in the wings. All of that extraneous stuff. ✶

BLVR: They're so beautiful.

ND: Every piece of sea glass is completely done, you know what I mean?

BLVR: They're so soft.

ND: The blues are quite rare. They remind me of when you read about Crete or something—the colors are so incredible. They're all from walks on beaches through my lifetime. There's a beach on Angel Island that is a fantastic glass beach. It's one of those places where there was an immigration station, like on Ellis Island. I got my insulator collection before the internet, so I don't know what it's worth. There's a magazine the collectors put out about them that lists the values for them, and so on.

BLVR: Just for insulators?

ND: Of course! Yeah, in fact, some of the insulator magazine issues are quite dear.

BLVR: Your insulators are unbelievably beautiful.

ND: I could not afford my insulator collection at this point. Some of the insulators are intentionally colored. This company intentionally made them blue because they were sharing the poles with another company.

BLVR: This insulator has such an unusual shape.

ND: Yeah, that's French. If these were all people on an airplane and someone said, *There are two people from Paris here*, you'd pick those.

BLVR: Amazing. That's true.

ND: They're very happy here in the windows—they get hot during the day and they warm the apartment… and you can also conduct them.

BLVR: With what?

ND: A baton. [*Laughs*] Now it's a full chorus—it takes about fifteen minutes. The sun comes around in the building and then the light shines through the first one, and then over fifteen minutes, this chord opens up.

BLVR: That's amazing. Did you ever make any light organs or anything like that?

ND: Like a keyboard attached to the insulators? Well, in a sense, yeah.

BLVR: You do kind of conduct light with your films, anyway.

ND: I do. These insulators are very sexy. This insulator has something that kind of looks like semen swimming around in it. My most valuable insulator is this, a yellow one from a company called Diamond. When I saw that, I knew the money was fleeing my pockets. I saw it at an insulator convention. They have shows like comic-book shows, you know, like at a county fair. And I saw this and I said, "I'm powerless."

BLVR: You felt the money leaving you like a spirit.

ND: This one is what in the hobby they call "shows good." Meaning that it's damaged but you can hide it. I could never have afforded it if it weren't for that.

BLVR: I like that: it's very show-business language.

ND: You want to see the insulator magazine? It's called *Crown Jewels of the Wire*. It's gotten worse and worse over time, though, because of computer graphics. They used to be very homemade. When I first got it, it felt very much like something we would do in Cub Scouts.

BLVR: Oh, wow. [*Looking at* Crown Jewels of the Wire] It's sort of like a zine. Do they still make them?

ND: Yeah. I sent something in once and got it on the cover.

BLVR: Really?

ND: It features an image from [the Cathedral of] Saint John the Divine in New York. They have stained-glass windows dedicated to certain professions, and they have one showing a lineman going up a telephone pole with an insulator.

BLVR: Oh my gosh.

ND: You can see the one little insulator there on the pole.

BLVR: Wow, that's great.

ND: I was so proud that I got a cover. Being into insulators is like going to a sex club, because everyone agrees that these are interesting. You don't have to be apologetic. You know what I mean? Everyone's agreeing that this is worth gathering about.

BLVR: Yeah, you don't have to explain yourself.

ND: Oh, and then there was a rebellion. There was a group that wanted to have no more buying of insulators, only trading—that was their new morality. So a counter-magazine, an insulator magazine in opposition to *Crown Jewels of the Wire*, came out, called *The Rainbow Riders' Trading Post*.

BLVR: It was a war within the insulator community.

ND: Insulators are a very, very American thing. There's no insulator shows in San Francisco. You have to drive at least two hours outside the city.

BLVR: How did you get into them in the first place?

ND: Kids my age used to lie on the back seat of their car when their parents were going on a trip, and you'd watch the wires go *shoo, shoo, shoo* [*makes whooshing sound*]. Each of the telephone poles has insulators. You'd see these things shining in the sun and it was like these votive things out of reach, out of sight, pulling the energy down from the heavens. And they flashed by, and eventually that affected your marrow.

BLVR: It's great you remember having that experience. I'm fascinated by the editorial board of this insulator magazine. [*Looking at the table of contents of* Crown Jewels of the Wire]. This Carol McDougald seems to be the real queen…

ND: Well, at the time, the McDougalds, she and her husband, published the magazine and then they sold it to another couple. There's all sorts of stories in there about, you know, stopping to get gas in a place and there's an insulator for twenty-five cents that's worth thirty-eight thousand dollars. They have all sorts of stories about going to old glassworks and digging things up.

BLVR: Thirty-eight thousand dollars: wow. It's literally like finding jewels.

ND: *Crown Jewels of the Wire*, yeah. Photographs don't do them justice. You know what's the best time to photograph insulators? On a dark, rainy day. They look so beautiful on a dark day. Unlike most collections, which just exist in boxes, these are actively joy-giving. It's not like you're just collecting baseball cards.

BLVR: I'd love to get into them.

ND: If someone goes nuts for them, then I respect them. If they say, *Oh, those look like dicks or something*… I mean, what does a dick look like? A dick looks like an insulator. [*Laughs*]

IV. PEN PALS

BLVR: You're friends with Peter? [*Points to photo of Nathaniel, Jerome, and Peter Lamborn Wilson, a.k.a. Hakim Bey*]

ND: Yeah.

BLVR: I live in Woodstock, so I knew Peter.

ND: When we took that photo, he had moved to Saugerties, New York. We were very fortunate, because many years ago, Jerome and Peter and I were made roommates, by chance, at Naropa [Institute]. It's a funny story—one of the reasons we went to Naropa to teach was because there was going to be a national insulator convention in Denver. So that was the real reason we were there! But I said to Jerome, "Sh, don't

tell anyone." But we told Pete we were going to an insulator convention, and he just sat there and made a prune face. Later that day, we came home with this gorgeous insulator and he says, "Hmm." He was a slow melt; he goes, "They are kind of charming." And then, "Are you going back tomorrow? Can I come?" [*Laughs*]

BLVR: That's hilarious. I mean, it seems right up his alley.

ND: I got him a bunch over the years.

BLVR: Now I keep seeing insulators in different objects all around the apartment…

ND: You're going mad! [*Laughs*]

BLVR: For instance, where's this painting of an insulator from?

ND: Oh! That was a gift from Piero. [*Laughs*] No, I'm kidding. I'll explain: An aunt had given me a bar mitzvah

---

FAKE MOVIE TITLES FROM *SEINFELD*

✷ *Means to an End*
✷ *Blame It on the Rain*
✷ *Rochelle, Rochelle*
✷ *Checkmate*
✷ *Sack Lunch*
✷ *Ponce de León*
✷ *Prognosis Negative*
✷ *Blimp: The Hindenburg Story*
✷ *The Pain and the Yearning*
✷ *Chow Fun*
✷ *Brown-Eyed Girl*
✷ *Firestorm*
✷ *Cupid's Revival*
✷ *Agent Zero*
✷ *Chunnel*

—list compiled by Bryce Woodcock

present of a photo by Margaret Bourke-White and it was hanging above the refrigerator there. Then one day, the poet Larry Fagin was visiting from New York and they left *The New York Times* on the couch and I looked down at it and it was the Sotheby's auctions, which were saying Margaret Bourke-White prints were selling for fifty-five thousand dollars. So I walked into the kitchen and went, Oh, it's fifty-five thousand dollars on the wall above the refrigerator. So I got it sold around 1990, and Jerome and I took a trip all around Italy. There's a town called Ravenna, which is famous for mosaics: it's where the Roman Empire descended to around the six or seven hundreds. Anyway, there's a church outside Ravenna called [the Basilica of Sant'Apollinare in] Classe, and there was a teenage boy who was working in the card department and he came up to Jerome and me and said, "I want to practice my English. Can I have your address?" And we have been writing each other to this day.

BLVR: Wow.

ND: And so he, at one point, like a good pen pal, asked, "What are your hobbies?" Universal pen pal question. So I wrote back, and I said, "This is gonna sound strange, blah, blah, blah, but I collect these things called insulators." So he began to go to flea markets in Italy, and occasionally he'd send us one. Anyway, he likes to paint and do crafts, so that's where that painting comes from. He also did the clock in the kitchen.

BLVR: Oh my god, the clock is amazing, also with insulators!

ND: Yeah, of course. [*Laughs*]

BLVR: That's fantastic. How long ago did you start writing to him?

ND: 1990.

BLVR: Wow.

ND: There's a mosaic over there that he also did.

BLVR: I was noticing that.

ND: He did that.

BLVR: That's really great. Has he ever come to visit?

ND: No, but he was almost a teenager then… Now he must be seventy or something.

BLVR: That's what happens.

ND: Unfortunately, now there's email.

BLVR: Oh, is that what you do now with him?

ND: Yeah, but always a package will come from Italy…

BLVR: Wow. That's so sweet.

ND: Yeah, email for pen pals is not ideal. FaceTime I enjoy, I have to confess. I like it because you don't have to talk; you can just smile at each other simply—it's a way of feeling a heart connection.

V. "THE ODDEST THING"

BLVR: How did you begin your work on *Dialogues*?

ND: Before starting work on *Dialogues*, I had no film to make, but I wanted to do something, so at a certain point I decided to just start, and it became a portrait of what the San Francisco summer is like.

BLVR: What is it like? I've never been here in the summer.

ND: There's no summer. [*Laughs*]

BLVR: When did you finish *Dialogues*?

ND: I think it was shot in June [2022]. I kept the fog at a discreet ratio, but in the film there is kind of a face-off, somehow, between the life force and—I don't know what you call it, the other one—oblivion?

BLVR: While watching it, I felt a kind of void, but one that I wanted to fall into.

ND: I think you can feel it's a film made by an older person. I don't mean that it's old-fashioned or stodgy; I mean there's a lot of death in it. Shakespeare has a line from *The Tempest* about being older, where every third thought is of death. It's such a great line. *Dialogues* feels a little like that feeling.

BLVR: But it's a beautiful depiction of it, and you made the void feel soft, in a way.

ND: I didn't kick you into a muddy hole?

BLVR: When you first cut onto that angled shot of the ocean, where the screen is all dark and there's just this glowing white swirl on the top, that completely knocked me out. It was very surprising. I love being put into that kind of place of confusion, which I think gets you into that void kind of place, but in a very beautiful way. In this film, the way the images are talking to each other throughout gives me a very fluid sense of time. How do you think about time when you're cutting?

ND: Film is like music: it creates its own time. It's the oddest thing.

BLVR: It's such a beautiful film, and quite sculptural, painterly, and musical. It's really like all the art forms in one.

ND: That's fair. I don't mean that I'm uniquely capable of that; I just mean that is the nature of cinema—it fits. Would you like to see another film? This one's more like generic Nathaniel…

BLVR: Please. [*Nathaniel screens* Place d'or.]

ND: So this one, *Place d'or*, came from a couple of afternoons at North Lake in Golden Gate Park. I was there and it was a kind of a drizzly gray autumn day and the trees were trying to be cheery and it

touched me in the way seasonal things are touching, and I just kind of went for it. You know, it's expensive to make a film, but it's good for me; it's good for my mind to do it. The problem-solving—I enjoy it very much.

BLVR: I felt like for so much of it, I was looking through three different planes. There were the leaves closest to me and then the landscape behind it and then an echo of humanity in the background with the car, and then there were a couple shots with people passing through the landscape.

ND: I mean, normally you would want to eliminate the cars because it's distracting, but I was somehow touched by them; they were sort of like arrows flying through the image.

BLVR: Yes. The cars were glimmering silver forms. It was a nice silver-and-gold moment.

ND: Yeah, so I didn't mind the cars. I mean, if someone wants to complain… [*Laughs*]

BLVR: It was magnificent. In some of those Piero paintings we were looking at, gold is such a powerful presence too.

ND: That's true—there's a thing you can't see in the reproductions of the paintings, but if you went to London to the National Gallery to see [Piero's] *The Baptism of Christ*, you'd see he has this beautiful little gold dust in the paint coming down through the tree. It's totally unphotographable. It's like what you might do with a fresco, where you apply the wet plaster and the mineral would make a sparkle.

BLVR: I'm gonna have to pilgrimage.

ND: Of course. It's fun to see them in situ, in Italy, but that's a big project. And at the National Gallery, they have nice sandwiches.

BLVR: And that makes it all come together. [*Laughs*]

ND: Yeah, and they're not those prissy little English sandwiches. ✶

REVEL

ATSURO RILEY, EDITOR IN CHIEF

Amit Majmudar   A.E. Stallings      Amy Gerstler   Shane McCrae

Ange Mlinko   Willard Spiegelman   Hugh Raffles   Jesse Nathan

Terrance Hayes   Stephanie Burt   **1**   Brenda Hillman   Stamatis Polenakis

Cal Bedient   Peter Campion   Devin Johnston   Bernard Cooper

Danielle Chapman   Kay Ryan   Hailey Leithauser   Natalie Shapero

Kwame Dawes   Christian Wiman   Randall Mann   Tom Thompson

Andrea Cohen   Tishani Doshi   Susan Unterberg   Joy Williams

Linda Gregerson   Forrest Gander   Chris Campanioni   Alan Thomas

Lucy Corin

IN PRINT FALL 2023
revel-literary.com

THE NEW ANIMALS

BY PIP ADAM

Pip Adam's *The New Animals* is a claustrophobic satire that dissects modern life with an unflinching eye. Set in 2016, the novel takes place over the course of a single day in Auckland, New Zealand, following a group of fashion-industry workers—designers, pattern-makers, stylists, hairdressers—as they prepare for a last-minute photo shoot.

At the center of the novel is Carla, a forty-three-year-old hairdresser who has spent too much of her life in fashion and is indignant that she has ended up working for a bunch of wealthy, entitled millennial designers. However, Carla's acerbic interior monologues bely a deeper sense of existential disconnection. Tommy, the visionary that heads the clothing label and employs Carla, constantly seeks Carla's approval while also feeling responsible for fixing the mess left by Carla's generation: "The planet was dying, there was poverty. This was what they'd left them."

The thread of fashion is woven throughout *The New Animals*, with Adam noting the perversity of how we decide what is fashionable and gently skewering the millennial designers' almost painful sincerity about their work. Yet she also maintains a reverence and respect for the art of fashion, inviting us at one point to appreciate the beauty in a simple white T-shirt: "The cotton had a nylon mix in it and the fabric fell long and still. It was so white as well. Like Jesus-in-heaven white… She loved the sleeves on it. The sleeves were a fucking revelation." Ultimately, however, we are left unsettled by the consumerist, disposable nature of fashion and its devastating ecological impact, a fact that becomes increasingly impossible to ignore.

Divided by generation and class, Adam's characters are quietly at war not only with one another—their conversations are rife with hidden meanings and misinterpretations—but also with themselves, often taking stabs at their own disappointing traits: "She was lazy. Really. That's what it always came down to. Too lazy to succeed, really. In any real way." The one exception is Elodie, the young "dumb nice" makeup artist, whom everyone appears to be sleeping with but no one seems to actually understand.

As Carla walks around Auckland, having meetings, cutting hair, and brimming with Gen X cynicism, she reflects on a city in constant flux: "She'd lived in Auckland for forty-three years and it still wasn't finished. Nothing stayed in place." Adam also floods the text with hyper-specific geographical details, describing Auckland with the same offhanded familiarity as another writer might London or New York. We sense that this once-quaint New Zealand town, previously a haven from the overpopulated global metropolises of the world, is now suffocating under the pressure of its own self-importance—it is a rapidly gentrifying city, now itself overpopulated and unsustainable.

The day wears on, and Carla's entire life seems to be teetering on the edge of collapse. The threats feel at once looming—her career may soon be drying up, her one close friendship is dissolving, her flat is almost unlivable—and imminent: her neglected pit bull, Doug, is homicidal, and their interactions are becoming more hostile by the day. "They were pitched against each other. Only one of them would walk away from this. Carla had the upper hand, literally—opposable thumbs, bipedal locomotion, technology—but Doug had teeth and was only muscle."

In the final third of the novel, Adam sheds the constraints of social realism and the narrative is transformed into a kind of oceanic dystopian fever dream. A less ambitious, less confident writer might not want to disorient their readers with such experimentation. But Adam would rather have us experience these ideas and be inundated by them than simply read about them. That sense of inescapability—from class, from the oceans we are polluting, from the future—is at the heart of *The New Animals*, and it all leads to the same place: "Everything that came to the ocean came for a reason. Some of it stayed, some of it was just passing through. But everything ended up here in the sea." —*Clara Sankey*

Publisher: *Dorothy, a publishing project* **Page count:** *272* **Price:** *$16.95* **Key quote:** *"They care too much. They care crazily about things that no one gives a fuck about—or should. That was why they ran the world."* **Shelve next to:** *Janet Frame, Dorthe Nors, Catherine Lacey* **Unscientifically calculated reading time:** *One luxuriously long hair appointment, waiting for the foils to set*

Illustration by Pete Gamlen

BATHHOUSE AND OTHER TANKA

BY TATSUHIKO ISHII, TRANSLATED BY HIROAKI SATO

Bathhouse and Other Tanka is Tatsuhiko Ishii's first volume of poetry translated into English. In *Bathhouse and Other Tanka* and in my lived experience, the bathhouse is a confounding place of both intimacy and distance. Here, in this church of public nakedness, we expose our bodies to one another. This is a kind of radical vulnerability, a way of being at our most undefended among strangers, a sentiment that resounds in Ishii's stripped-down prose. Still, when confronted with the sag, snap, and shape of another, one realizes that seeing someone nude doesn't mean you know anything about them. If anything, the mystery of the other deepens. That scar running down a woman's calf, the series of pockmarks on another's arm: all of these point to an interior that is simultaneously brandished and held away.

Such is the world of *Bathhouse and Other Tanka*. In one poem, written as an elegy for Genji from Murasaki Shikibu's *The Tale of Genji*, Ishii writes, "I sorrow over his heart deep in amorous attachments. Of what a / man ought to be (a human ought to be)." In these poems, ephemera wreathe convictions on how one ought to live. We see glimpses into the speaker's heart, only to be pushed back and offered a description of romance or nature. In another poem, this time written as an elegy for Yukio Mishima, the speaker flits between interjections of the "Dies irae" in Latin and meditations on yearning for death while remaining alive. Sacred Catholic language provides artifice, while alternately obscuring frank glimpses into the suicidal thoughts Ishii offers and takes away, rocking readers between crystalline sentiments and foggy anomie.

In these poems, the give-and-take of intimacy and distance is specifically attached to the society of men: inviolate fathers, murderous sons, and lithe male prostitutes. *Bathhouse* strives to articulate taut and slanted relationships between men who love and hate one another in equal measure. Lust sits alongside apathy, with speakers as prone to musing as to murder:

> To clear Father, his soiled name…. Looked after
>> by my son in a
> previous life, and, dying
>
> Whoever he may be, the son is a patricide…
> Looking
>> up at the
> peak soaring black in the predawn dark

Speakers also voice homoerotic admiration:

> The soul's (fragile) armor? The young man's (smooth
>> and cool)
> body in the buff

There is no linear through line driving its way through these poems, no thesis about the way men ought to be with one another. Instead, there is only the passive togetherness of the bathhouse, of these male bodies that exist wetly next to one another, mired in their own musing.

Undergirding this society of men is the poetic form Ishii writes in: the tanka. The tanka is a classical form of Japanese poetry that breaks its lines into a 5-7-5-7-7 syllable count. I was taught about the tanka alongside its cousin, the haiku, in American creative writing classes, where the form was presented to me as a syllable-counting game, a mere word puzzle to be solved on one's fingers. Ishii's tanka do not exist as little blurbs bounded by trite rules, but rather in long, heady sequences, the overall effect of which serves to highlight the swirling contemplation of love, loss, desire, and disgust he conjures. After all, during the Heian period, tanka were used as a form of communication between lovers. Ishii's tanka retain some of that ancient veneer, agony obfuscated by apathy, the body of the beloved, just out of damp reach.

—*Nina Li Coomes*

Publisher: *New Directions* **Page count:** *160* **Price:** *$18.95* **Key quote:** *"Deep at night a big incident! My heart taken by a small-framed, / skinny, little shit / Yet another incident? The boy I've picked up has a dimple (and a scar) / on his cheek."* **Shelve next to:** *Garth Greenwell, Yukio Mishima, Alexander Chee, Murasaki Shikibu, Chen Chen* **Unscientifically calculated reading time:** *Four long soaks plus three bursts while waiting for the shower to heat up*

Illustration by Pete Gamlen

TOUCHING THE ART

When I was a young queer making my way through the early aughts, the anthologies of Mattilda Bernstein Sycamore transformed my life and the lives of those around me. In college we passed around *That's Revolting: Queer Strategies for Resisting Assimilation* and *Nobody Passes: Rejecting the Rules of Gender and Conformity* like dumpstered lumber that scaffolded new ways of imagining our survival in the world—where being queer was necessarily an identity, a politic, and an ideology.

Touching the Art, Sycamore's sixth book as a solo author, is a memoir/history that unpacks her relationship with her late visual artist grandmother, the abstract artist Gladys Goldstein—although in this case the notion of solo authorship may be a bit of a misnomer. Perhaps inspired by Sycamore's early work as an anthologist, this book blurs the lines of genre convention and polyvocality by assembling a multivoiced collage of texture, feeling, and evidence. Sycamore works with archival materials, resuscitated and reconstructed memory, and interviews to produce a collection that's part art history, part art theory, and part memoir, collapsing the spaces between authorship and authority, and between knowledge production and inheritance.

The book opens with a bouquet of chiasmi—a literary figuration where a phrase is written and then repeated in its reverse order to reveal something true buried inside the sentence—offering up aphorisms about the relationship between art, the self, and the world. She writes, "If art is a gap in feeling, it's also a feeling of the gap." These reflective gestures, on a sentence level, mirror both the serpentine unfolding of memory that takes place over the course of the book as well as the geometric logic that structures abstract painting.

Often ekphrastic, Sycamore offers multiple entry points into the visual landscape of her grandmother's work.

Publisher: *Soft Skull Press* **Page count:** *304* **Price:** *$27.00* **Key quote:** *"Art is always a mystery, even when it's not a mystery. How it affects us, or fails to. How we fail. How art fails us."* **Shelve next to:** *Sarah Schulman, Hilton Als, Douglas Crimp, David Wojnarowicz* **Unscientifically calculated reading time:** *Two packs of cigarettes, one reckless flirtation, and a lovely day at Mountain View Cemetery*

Sycamore paints with language, using it as device to translate her grandmother's canvases into multisensory descriptions that branch off into various sites of memory, analysis, and juxtaposed quotations, modeling how inseparable art and life are. "Pathways of mauve, cobalt, aquamarine, gray and red and purple hues. It's those chains again, this time in paint, connecting me to you." The book invites the reader to put down the collection and reconsider their relationship to the visual world at large, and to the book they're holding as an art object.

The spine of *Touching the Art* is an exploration of the author's complex and multidimensional relationship with her grandmother. And yet the modular, wide-ranging, and lyric structure, which echoes some of the formal work of Sycamore's previous book, *The Freezer Door*, makes an argument that in order to fully touch any experience, it is essential to view it within its wider and more diffuse context. Thus, the book is built from narratives of her life with her grandmother, marginalia from her grandmother's life and work, the gendered politics of abstract expressionism, familial homophobia, the history of Baltimore, racialized violence and white flight, desire and estrangement. By collaging these various fragments together, Sycamore offers a truer, more dynamic living portrait and makes a claim about queer time and geography that challenges us to push against notions of linearity and inherited borders.

The book's title, *Touching the Art*, also resonates on multiple levels. It is both one person's attempt at getting closer to a person and the art form they worked in, and it is asking us, the reader, to do this as well. It asks us to place our hand and tongue directly on the painting, to know that it becomes ours through this contact, and that both we and the artwork will be changed by our touch.

—*Sam Sax*

IF I CLOSE MY EYES

BY BEN FAMA

Nothing says twenty-first-century contemporary America like the convergence of reality TV, a mass shooting, and instant celebrity. This is precisely the scene where poet Ben Fama's first novel, *If I Close My Eyes*, begins. Enter Jesse Shore on his nineteenth birthday, while passing his gap year working retail in Manhattan, as he waits in line at Kim Kardashian's book signing at 555 Fifth Avenue. Cameras are rolling as anti-fur protesters surge, followed by gunshots, which "almost sounded cute, like snapping bubble wrap." This kind of juxtaposition of horror and cuteness trails Jesse throughout the book. One person is killed; another, Marsy-Rose Arenas, is grazed; and Jesse ends up in the hospital for a few weeks. As he comes to, film crews are setting up in his room: enter the Kardashians, Kanye, and producer Ryan Seacrest.

The absurdity inherent to this juncture of violence and Kardashians with cameras rolling has been present since the nascence of reality TV, which first blossomed after the OJ Simpson Bronco chase. Kardashian patriarch Robert read Simpson's suicide note to ninety-five million viewers. This, more than a decade before E!'s *Keeping Up with the Kardashians* (*KUWTK*) debuted, a show that you *know* even if you've never seen an episode. The docusoap thrives on the ebb and flow of interpersonal drama. It's the same chaos that brings together Jesse and Marsy-Rose (also known as Mars)—a natural beauty and aspiring though steadily B-list actress—as both attempt to parlay their fleeting visibility into something more lasting.

Something more lasting takes the form of many ideas: creating a spin-off show with Jesse and Mars; filing suit based on a theory that the protest and shooting were instigated by the show; becoming paid representatives in campaigns against gun violence. One might think they would bond over their shared trauma, but truly it's over their desire for capital—cultural and financial. Of course, Jesse swoons over Mars's beauty and is also drawn to her wildness. He's a willing sidekick, too, indulging and partaking in her substance-fueled dramas. Mars is attracted to her melancholy young admirer and his clever ideas. It's the LA fever dream of a television drama. It's the putrid LA sunshine of *Tangerine*. It's the addled LA of Jon Lindsey's *Body High*, and at times the addictively vapid and beguiling LA of *KUWTK*.

For a story so chaotic that pops with the banter and name-dropping of a social media feed, *If I Close My Eyes* has a surprisingly conventional structure. Fama is the author of two poetry books, *Fantasy* and *Deathwish*. Both are linguistically playful, steeped in the moment, and pursue similar obsessions to *If I Close My Eyes*, but they read as if they were dashed off, an insignia of élan. The novel is a completely different project. Fictional tabloid clips and *New York Times* profiles (Fama nails the style) are folded within the narrative, and yet the storylines are continuous. Jesse pines for Mars, Jesse relapses, Jesse resists his self-destructive impulses. Ultimately, the narrative circles back to the Kardashians, to a resolution where the reader can witness how Jesse and Mars are both moving forward in their lives. But maybe this is a red herring. Jesse often points out the red herrings in dramas, including in his mother's Emmy-nominated series and in *KUWTK*: "[The] family drama was a red herring: the conflict is the desire for more screen time against the fickle antagonism of the viewership, the passing time that ebbs and flows the ratings toward and away from high-res horizons."

Jesse's realization of the family drama as a red herring points the reader toward Fama's machinations within the novel, and to ask what is so compelling about this narrative—only to find, with both admiration and cynicism, that the story is deployed to engross. When done well, the reader is rapt and complicit in these age-old tropes. It's Fama's meta-textual nod toward the contrivances of a novel, to the act of author as auteur. By turning the mirror, Fama provokes further inquiry into the nature of our own obsessions.

—*Anne K. Yoder*

Publisher: *SARKA* **Page count:** *170* **Price:** *$20.00* **Key quote:** *"Jesse felt a paranoid wave that the shooting and subsequent attention were part of a Faustian deal Mars had made to become more famous by way of the incident, he and the dead woman the collateral damage of her career path."* **Shelve next to:** *Kate Durbin, Jon Lindsey, Robert Ashley* **Unscientifically calculated reading time:** *Five dermal filler appointments*

Illustration by Pete Gamlen

THE DELIVERY

BY MARGARITA GARCÍA ROBAYO

The Delivery, a new novel by Colombian writer Margarita García Robayo, presents the world of an expatriate writer, a Colombian in Buenos Aires who dreams of finishing a novel. Our unnamed protagonist juggles an intractable lover, a ghostly mother, a disturbed cat, and a slew of disgruntled neighbors. She is a writer at odds with her materials, like "a carpenter who is allergic to sawdust," at once totally enamored with language and certain that "everything told is damaged." To make ends meet, she works apathetically as a copywriter, crafting marketing language for a company that produces humanely raised beef. As the days and weeks pass, a slew of packages arrives from her sister back in Colombia, filling her apartment to the brim with objects of varying significance. In the meantime, for a good portion of the book, she waits.

In the meantime—perhaps the true setting of Robayo's novel, more than Buenos Aires, is the meantime, the time of expectancy and of ideation—Robayo's protagonist is waiting for a family secret, for a lover's call, for a friend's response, for life-shifting news. Waiting, she eddies inside wonder. The novel illustrates a thinking mind, a mind met with delay, a mind that is merciless and ever turning inward. Such minds tend to fold in on themselves: "Inaugurating a body or a house is to commence its deterioration... deterioration, I think now, is a superior state of matter because it means something has flourished in it. Only that which has given fruit can rot." These sentences, and the idea they house, express one motor of Robayo's craft: she is a writer as fascinated by rot as by ripeness, and especially by the clouded border between the two.

The secret aspiration of any expatriate is to be past-less. Crossing a border—into a new grammar, a new cuisine, a new flora, a new backdrop for living—creates a crease in a life. Expatriates, unlike immigrants, hope such a crease will allow for a clean tear. Robayo's protagonist is no different:

> **Publisher:** *Charco Press* **Page count:** *169* **Price:** *$16.95* **Key quote:** *"Parents are the peephole you look through to spy on your childhood."* **Shelve next to:** *Magda Szabó, Marieke Lucas Rijneveld, Jennifer Croft* **Unscientifically calculated reading time:** *Two or three hazy morning reading sessions, when you wake up early but the person beside you in bed is still asleep*

she wants to tuck her family, and her life before Argentina, out of sight. At the same time, she is painfully aware of how our histories create us: "When someone is born," she determines, "they debut old features, they come with a burden of past that will always be greater than their future." At another moment, she admits: "I have a collection of childhood accidents stored up in my body." Inside the music of Robayo's prose, one encounters an argument about the vigor of personal history, its relentless capacity to emboss the present.

"Our ability to fool ourselves is infinite," writes Robayo at another moment. Reading this novel, I thought often about the common wish for everything in life to attain significance. Each love, each glance, the smell of eucalyptus, the printed inscription on a delivered package. Are we fooling ourselves to think this? If all the details in our lives eventually achieve meaning, nothing can be discarded; nothing can be overlooked. Meaning (of all kinds) produces grief, but only meaninglessness produces despair.

I believe, above all else, that *The Delivery* is a book about meaninglessness, about splintered meanings, a book about misinterpretation and the abyss. To Robayo's eye, we will never close the misunderstandings between one another: "Every person is a nucleus bordered by gaps of incomprehension. Even those who feel the closest to us are separated by that thin but deep edge." At the close of the book, Robayo departs from the reader mid-breath, neglecting to deliver to us some culminating event that would corral all the book's various dramas into one unified shape. We are left in awe of this novel's intellectual exercise, and with a furious hope that such an exercise might return to its own starting place, forming a perfect circle. But "a return, almost always, is a failure," Robayo reminds us. Chekhov's gun remains unfired. The circle stays open. A life, arbitrarily, carries on.

—*Ricardo Frasso Jaramillo*

Illustration by Pete Gamlen

THE PUZZLE OF INCREDIBLY WIDE AND DEEP KNOWLEDGE

IF YOU COMPLETE THIS PUZZLE, YOU ARE A GENERALIST OF BROAD SKILL AND GREAT RENOWN

by Wyna Liu; edited by Benjamin Tausig

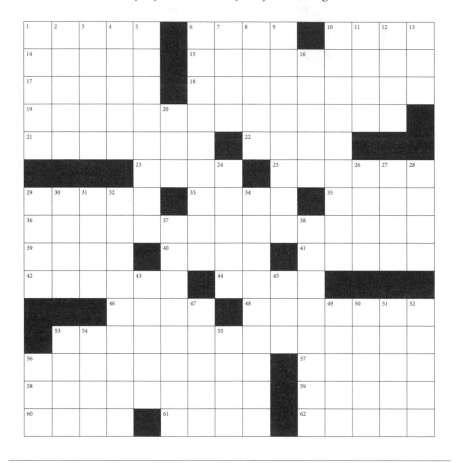

ACROSS

1. Cutting-edge athletic gear
6. Pole, e.g.
10. Cadre ___ (beverage sponsor in "The Running Man")
14. How some beer is served
15. It has rules for writing
17. Italian musical direction appropriated by Little Richard
18. Longtime music magazine based at Lincoln Center
19. Source of original pirate material
21. What Forum ruins demarcate
22. Level in Maslow's hierarchy
23. ___ Punk
25. Full of toppings, on a menu
29. TV series whose theme was Massive Attack's "Teardrop"
33. Home to the lake monster Bessie
35. One with a ridiculous rider, perhaps
36. Question about a chair's status?
39. Jocundity
40. Couple of people?
41. Only quadruped whose front legs are longer than its back legs
42. [Fingers crossed emoji]
44. ___ gin (liqueur that isn't technically a gin)
46. So
48. Appetizer served with an empty bowl
53. Expression that occurs just once, such as "honorificabilitudinitatibus" in Shakespeare's canon
56. Sign of no return?
57. "It's too haaaaard"
58. Do some quiet quitting
59. Less likely to volunteer, in a way
60. Juniors, say
61. Gave the once-over
62. Like some game-time decisions, necessarily

DOWN

1. Italian musical direction never appropriated by Little Richard
2. It might help you get a grip on motorcycle riding
3. Addressed on Twitter, casually
4. Turkic language with Kazan and Mishar dialects
5. What a pilot might become
6. Event that might get some nods from the audience?
7. Gait that resembles a canter
8. Heated up some leftovers, say
9. Little poem
10. Annual July 1 or 2 event commemorating the Constitution Act of 1867
11. One side of a store sign
12. NSFW
13. ___ longa, vita brevis
16. Extreme throwback diet
20. She played June in "Henry & June"
24. They're pretty sticky!
26. Flood protection
27. Like any whole number doubled
28. "O, ___" (Big Star song with the lyric "she's got a magic wand that says play with yourself before other ones")
29. Word with five or priest
30. Capital nicknamed the "Tiger City" despite not having any tigers
31. Sch. that's home to Sun Bowl stadium
32. They get baked
34. Postapocalyptic Richard Matheson novel that inspired "Night of the Living Dead"
37. Punk pioneer whose first band was named for a 1970 Vincent Price movie, familiarly
38. Non-"English" people, collectively
43. Most abundant of the sedimentary rocks
45. Shape-shifter on "Deep Space Nine"
47. Bluish gray
49. Manga genre divided into "super robot" and "real robot" subgenres
50. Nin who wrote "Henry and June"
51. En plein air painter
52. Logger's output
53. Ritz-adjacent
54. "Beowulf" poet, e.g., for short
55. Saab or Tahari of fashion
56. Film resolution inits.

(answers on page 116)

COPYEDITING THE CLASSICS

SP /S ⑩ ERRORS HAVE BEEN INERTED INTO THIS PASSAGE. CAN YOU FIND THEM ?

by Caitlin Van Dusen

I KNOW WHY THE CAGED BIRD SINGS (1969)
by MAYA ANGELOU

It occurred to me that she expected a response. The sweet, vanilla flavor was still on my tongue and her reading was a wonder in my ears. I had to speak.

I said, "Yes ma'am." It was the least I could do, but it was the most also.

"There's one more thing. Take this book of poems and memorize one for me. Next time you pay me a visit, I want you to recite."

I have tried often to search behind the sophistication of years for the enchantment I so easily found in those gifts. The essence escapes but its aura remains. To be allowed, no, invited, into the private lives of strangers, and to share their joys and fears was a chance to exchange the southern bitter wormwood for a cup of mead with *Beowulf* or a hot cup of tea and milk with Oliver Twist. When I said aloud, "It is a far, far better thing that I do, than I have ever done…" Tears of love filled my eyes at my selflessness.

On that first day, I ran down the hill and into the road (few cars ever came along it) and had the good sense to stop running before I reached the Store.

I was liked, and what a difference it made. I was respected not as Mrs. Henderson's grandchild or Bailey's sister but for just being Marguerite Johnson.

Childhood's logic never asks to be proved (all conclusions are absolute). I didn't question why Mrs. Flowers had singled me out for attention, nor did it occur to me that Momma may have asked her to give me a little talking to. All I cared about was that she had made tea cookies for *me* and read to me from her favorite book. It was enough to prove that she liked me.

Momma and Bailey were waiting inside the Store. He said, "My, what did she give you?" He had seen the books, but I held the paper sack with his cookies in my arms shielded by the poems.

Momma sighed, "Sister, I know you acted like a little lady. That do my heart good to see settled people take to you all. I'm trying my best, the Lord knows, but these days—" Her voice trailed off. "Go on in and change your dress."

(answers on page 116)

Follow The Chicago Manual of Style, 17th edition. Please ignore unusual spellings, hyphenations, and capitalizations, and the that/which distinction. All are characteristic of the author's style and time.

JACKET CAPTCHA

CAN YOU IDENTIFY THESE NINE CLASSIC BOOK JACKETS?

COMPLETE ME

HOW WELL DO YOU KNOW JOY WILLIAMS?
FILL IN THIS PARAGRAPH OF BIOGRAPHICAL TRIVIA, PENNED BY THE AUTHOR HERSELF.

I grew up in _____. My father and grandfather were
both _____. As a young man, my grandfather won the
Welsh Eisteddfod Poetry Prize which was a hand-carved massively
ornate oak throne. This I wanted very much but he bequeathed it tp
the Wilkes Barre (Penna) Historical Society and it was _____.
I have always had _____ dogs. My first dog's name was _____.
I have _____ and _____ now. I also care for two _____.
Both are extremely attractive and personable. I once worked
for the U.S. _____ compiling the circumstances of _____.
I have nine _____ and ~~_____~~ two pairs of
_____. I once wrote a _____. And once, astonishingly, I owned
a 1960 _____.

CLASSIFIEDS

Believer Classifieds cost $2 per word. They can be placed by emailing classifieds@thebeliever.net. All submissions subject to editorial approval. No results guaranteed.

LISTEN UP

INTRODUCING FEELSING— A debut album of post-rock beats, grooves, and atmospheres for listeners and readers of all ages, by DJ Baby Chocolate. To listen to the album and other unique sound worlds, go to eartrumpetrecordings. bandcamp.com.

GUTSY RADIO—Seven nights a week of live, webcast, DJ-driven shows from across these United States. Two-hour volunteer slots of music and attitude. Community radio for all. This is not a test. gutsyradio.org

SERVICES

WE SWEAR BY CHEAP THERAPY! is a worker-owned, unionized printer and publisher. Seize the press and build with us. radixmedia.org.

CHANGE YOUR LIFE TODAY! futuretensebooks.com for Parker Young's debut collection of stories, *Cheap Therapist Says You're Insane*, and more.

WRITE UNBORING PLAYS—Classes, accountability, and consults for inquisitive, rebellious dramatists. Shake it up. katetarker.com

CARE TX RESCUE is a 501(c)3 saving shelter dogs in TX and rehoming them out of state. Don't miss the chance to meet your new best friend! See caretx.org/adoptable-dogs for more information.

MISSED CONNECTIONS

SEEKING—Man exiting the basement of the Strand sometime around midday with a friend, on June 15, 2023. I couldn't help but notice your haul, which featured a number of my favorites. Curious to know, when you read it: Did you like *Parallel Lives*? Please write back through this Classifieds page, if you see this. From a fellow bookworm, NANCY.

SUBMISSIONS

BEN AFFLECK WAS HERE— Potentially. Probably. Plausibly. *No Contact Magazine* is newly open for submissions in short-form fiction, nonfiction, poetry. Just think to yourself: Would Ben like this? More at nocontactmag.com.

ACTUALLY FREE

LITTLE ENGINES—a mid-brow magazine, free in print. Zero dollars, straight to your mailbox. You just have to ask: littleengines.pub

FELICITATIONS

CONGRATULATIONS on graduating from URI, Sara, and good luck with your new job at PepsiCo. I love you!

BON VOYAGE BUT NEVER GOODBYE—Our dearest Stacey, we miss you more than words can say, but we are so excited to read your letters and other dispatches from Europe, and to visit you very soon. Nabila's isn't the same without you. <3 YOUR WORMEN.

WE COULDN'T BE PROUDER of our MD-in-the-making, and new father to Fran, Jake! Forever Go Blue! <3 YOUR FAVORITE BROTHER.

TRADES

RECORDS/ART—Man who works at 849 Valencia St. and draws pictures of animals and mid-century philosophers would like to barter any vinyl records by John Edwards (later of the Spinners), or Roberta Flack (though not Quiet Fire). Send records to the address just mentioned, and you'll receive original artwork by this man previously mentioned.

PUBLICATIONS

ROUNDABOUT—the new debut novel by Will Mountain Cox, in which a group of friends and lovers in Paris weathers the polycrisis of contemporary life together, exploring cycles of connecting, belonging, departing, and inevitable change, as seasons turn and nights out give way to the pull of something more. To order, go to RelegationBooks.com.

IF YOUR BOOK IS A WEDGE IN A CRACK, Split/Lip Press is the hammer helping you split the wall apart. Use code SLPBELIEVER at splitlippress.com for 25% off your next order of boundary-breaking books and don't miss SISTER GOLDEN CALF, an unforgettable road trip story from debut author Colleen Burner.

ANNOUNCING THE FALL '23 DOROTHIES! Dorothy, a publishing project's 2023 titles: Kate Briggs's *The Long Form*, a novel about motherhood and the form of the novel, or novels and the forms of motherhood, and Pip Adam's *The New Animals*, a surrealist dive into the New Zealand fashion industry, class and generational conflict, and climate catastrophe. Available everywhere and at dorothyproject.com.

COST OF PAPER!—An unprintable publication. costofpaper.com.

WHY IS DORITOS COOL RANCH THE GOD-TIER CHIP?—Subscribe to LOOSEY at brendonholder.substack.com for biweekly essays on culture, technology, humanity, and all the crucial questions. Your group chat will thank you!

CHOO CHOO, MOTHERF*CKER—We're a small Risograph press publishing zines and chapbooks with an emphasis on obsession, nostalgia, and states of liminality. Say hi at choochoopress.com.

Illustrations by Tomi Um

INTERNATIONAL BESTSELLER LISTS

See what the rest of the world is reading in this regular feature, which highlights a rotating cast of countries in each issue.

COMPILED BY GINGER GREENE, ACCORDING TO 2022 ANNUAL LISTS

MEXICO

1. ***Todo lo que nunca fuimos (All That We Never Were)* by Alice Kellen.** *After her parents' deaths, the depressed Leah moves into the home of her brother's best friend, Axel, for whom she has long harbored feelings.*

2. ***Violeta* by Isabel Allende.** *On her deathbed during the COVID-19 pandemic, Violeta recounts the events of her hundred-year life.*

3. ***Todo lo que somos juntos (All That We Are Together)* by Alice Kellen.** *In the sequel to Todo lo que nunca fuimos, Leah's artistic success leads her to reunite with a heartbroken Axel when he becomes her agent.*

4. ***Un cuento perfecto (A Perfect Short Story)* by Elísabet Benavent.** *Unhappy as a powerful executive at her family's company, Margot and a bartender she just met go to Greece on a whim.*

5. ***Ciudades de humo (The City of Smoke)* by Joana Marcús.** *The twenty-one-year-old author first published this novel—about an android learning to blend in among humans—on the Wattpad platform.*

6. ***Las batallas en el desierto (Battles in the Desert)* by José Emilio Pacheco.** *In this novella originally serialized by the newspaper* Unomásuno, *a young boy falls in love with his best friend's mother.*

7. ***Cien años de soledad (One Hundred Years of Solitude)* by Gabriel García Márquez.** *A seminal work of magical realism that has been translated into forty-six languages and sold over fifty million copies.*

8. ***Pedro Páramo* by Juan Rulfo.** *A man visits the town of Comala and finds it populated by ghosts in this 1955 classic.*

9. ***Lascivia: pecados placenteros (Lust: Pleasurable Sins)* by Eva Muñoz.** *An army lieutenant becomes infatuated with the new colonel, despite his being her boyfriend's best friend.*

10. ***El peligro de estar cuerda (The Danger of Being Sane)* by Rosa Montero.** *An exploration of how creativity and mental illness are linked, told through a mix of essays and fiction.*

AUSTRALIA

1. ***Exiles* by Jane Harper.** *A detective returns to South Australian wine country, where a case involving an abandoned infant has yet to be solved.*

2. ***Lying Beside You* by Michael Robotham.** *A forensic psychologist is in the middle of a case when his brother returns from a psychiatric institution years after killing their parents.*

3. ***Cobalt Blue* by Matthew Reilly.** *Initially written as a screenplay, this novella imagines a world in which Russia and the United States are protected from nuclear war by superheroes from each country, until the American hero dies.*

4. ***The Dictionary of Lost Words* by Pip Williams.** *A lexicographer's daughter collects lost words in this story about the patriarchal origins of the Oxford English Dictionary.*

5. ***Apples Never Fall* by Liane Moriarty.** *A picture-perfect family of six is thrown into crisis after the mother disappears and the father is suspected of her murder.*

6. ***The Orphans* by Fiona McIntosh.** *The adopted daughter of an undertaker fights sexism as she endeavors to become Australia's first female mortician.*

7. ***Dirt Town* by Hayley Scrivenor.** *A young girl's disappearance creates problems for a tight-knit community in rural Australia.*

8. ***The Tilt* by Chris Hammer.** *Old bones continue to appear after a regulator explosion near the Murray River.*

9. ***Boy Swallows Universe* by Trent Dalton.** *In a gritty Brisbane suburb, a young boy takes care of his mute brother and dreams of becoming a journalist.*

10. ***Horse* by Geraldine Brooks.** *Spanning generations, this novel remembers a famous American racehorse and the enslaved Black equestrian who was key to his success.*

IRELAND

1. ***Again, Rachel* by Marian Keyes.** *A recovering addict working at a rehab center discovers that her ex-husband is back in town.*

2. ***Forever Home* by Graham Norton.** *In small-town Ireland, an unlikely relationship is challenged by protective family members and neighborhood gossip.*

3. ***Small Things Like These* by Claire Keegan.** *A well-liked man faces a moral dilemma when he discovers something disturbing about a local laundry led by nuns.*

4. ***The Queen of Dirt Island* by Donal Ryan.** *Spanning several generations, a family of women in rural Tipperary must depend on each other as they face life's trials.*

5. ***Once Upon a Time in… Donnybrook* by Ross O'Carroll-Kelly.** *The twenty-second book in a satirical series written by journalist Paul Howard, and published under the name of his infamous rugby-jock character.*

6. ***Normal People* by Sally Rooney.** *Two teenagers of different class backgrounds fall in love and begin school at Trinity College.*

7. ***Rachel's Holiday* by Marian Keyes.** *The prequel to Again, Rachel, this novel introduces us to the eponymous character on her to way to seek treatment following an overdose.*

8. ***All the Broken Places* by John Boyne.** *In the sequel to The Boy in the Striped Pyjamas, an old woman is haunted by memories of Nazi Germany when a new family moves into her building.*

9. ***Idol* by Louise O'Neill.** *Perspectives clash after an influencer writes about a sexual experience involving her former best friend.*

10. ***Beautiful World, Where Are You* by Sally Rooney.** *Two long-distant friends share emails on love, art, and politics as they enter new relationships and navigate adulthood.*

JAPAN

1. ***同志少女よ、敵を撃て (Comrade Girl, Shoot the Enemy)* by Aisaka Touma.** *A young girl trains as a sniper in the Red Army after her family is murdered by German soldiers during World War II.*

2. ***マスカレード・ゲーム (Masquerade Game)* by Keigo Higashino.** *A detective goes undercover as a hotel clerk in anticipation of another attack from a serial killer–at–large.*

3. ***その本は (The Book Is)* by Naoki Matayoshi and Shinsuke Yoshitake.** *Two men journey in search of stories for their book-loving king, who can no longer read.*

4. ***転生したらスライムだった件 (19) (That Time I Got Reincarnated as a Slime (19))* by Fuse.** *A middle-aged salaryman is reborn, spineless and blind, into a magical world.*

5. ***変な家 (Strange House)* by Rain Hole.** *A novelization of the hit YouTube video created by the author, who invariably appears in his films wearing a black suit and a white mask.*

6. ***オーバーロード(16) (Overlord (16))* by Kugane Maruyama.** *Originally published online, this series is set in the world of a massive multiplayer online role-playing game called YGGDRASIL.*

7. ***オーバーロード(15) (Overlord (15))* by Kugane Maruyama.** *The fifteenth book in the series features its skeleton protagonist, Ainz Ooal Gown, on a vacation in the Elf Country.*

8. ***黒牢城 (The Samurai and the Prisoner)* by Honobu Yonezawa.** *Four years before the Honnō-ji Incident of 1582, a mystery unfolds in Arioka Castle.*

9. ***夢をかなえるゾウ (Dream Elephant)* by Keiya Mizuno.** *The elephant god Ganesha proffers his wisdom in this comic self-help book.*

10. ***おいしいごはんが食べられますように (That You Might Eat Well)* by Junko Takase.** *A love triangle between three office workers is complicated by their differing opinions on food.*

NOTES ON OUR CONTRIBUTORS

Anika Banister is a writer and editor in Brooklyn, New York. She works for New York Review Books.

Nina Li Coomes is a Japanese and American writer currently living in Chicago.

Will Epstein is a composer, improviser, and songwriter born in New York City. He has performed internationally, released records of songs, and composed music for films, installations, and dance performances, including commissions for the Martha Graham Dance Company, the Metropolitan Museum of Art, the Joyce Theater, and the recent documentary *Nam June Paik: Moon Is the Oldest TV*. His albums *Whims* and *Wendy* were released by Fat Possum Records in 2022 and 2023, respectively.

Ricardo Frasso Jaramillo is a poet and writer. His work can be found in *The New York Times*, *McSweeney's Quarterly*, *The Rumpus*, and *The Adroit Journal*, among other venues. He currently teaches in the English Department of the Universidad Nacional Autónoma de México, in Mexico City.

Katie Gee Salisbury is the author of *Not Your China Doll: The Wild and Shimmering Life of Anna May Wong*, a biography of the first Asian American movie star, which is forthcoming from Dutton in March 2024. Her work has appeared in *The New York Times*, *Vanity Fair*, *The Ringer*, the Asian American Writers' Workshop, and elsewhere. She also writes the newsletter *Half-Caste Woman*.

Teddy Goldenberg was born in Israel in 1985. He lives in Berlin with his wife, the artist Noa Münster. His most recent book, *City Crime Comics*, was released by Floating World Comics. He is currently at work on a sequel called *The Retirement Party*.

Ginger Greene is a writer from Toronto.

Ken Howe is a practicing dermatologist in New York City. He has been collecting (and reading, he swears!) books for nearly four decades. His Instagram account, @constantreader17, recounts his book-searching adventures. His writing has appeared in *Mr. Beller's Neighborhood*. He lives in Brooklyn, New York, with his family and approximately eight thousand books.

Jordan Kisner is the author of the essay collection *Thin Places: Essays from In Between*, named one of NPR's best books of 2020. She is a contributing writer for *The New York Times Magazine* and *The Atlantic*, and her work has appeared in *n+1*, *The Paris Review*, *The Guardian*, *The American Scholar*, *The Best American Essays 2016*, and elsewhere. She is also the creator and host of *Thresholds*, a Literary Hub podcast. She lives in New York.

Maris Kreizman is a writer and critic and the host of *The Maris Review*, a literary podcast. Her essay collection, *I Want to Burn This Place Down*, is forthcoming from HarperCollins.

Amy Kurzweil is a *New Yorker* cartoonist and the author of *Flying Couch: A Graphic Memoir* and *Artificial: A Love Story* (October 2023). Amy was a 2021 Berlin Prize Fellow at the American Academy in Berlin and a 2019 Shearing Fellow at the Black Mountain Institute, and has received fellowships from MacDowell, Djerassi, and elsewhere. Her work has been nominated for a Reuben Award, and an Ignatz Award for *Technofeelia*, her four-part graphic series with this magazine. Her writing, comics, and cartoons have also been published in *The Verge*, *The New York Times Book Review*, *Longreads*, *Literary Hub*, *Wired*, and many other places. Amy teaches a monthly cartooning class online, open to the public, via her Patreon.

Cathy Linh Che is a Vietnamese American writer and multidisciplinary artist. She is the author of *Split* (Alice James Books) and coauthor, with Kyle Lucia Wu, of the children's book *An Asian American A to Z: A Children's Guide to Our History* (Haymarket Books). She is working on a poetry manuscript, a creative nonfiction manuscript, a video installation, and a short documentary, with director Christopher Radcliff, on her parents' experiences as refugees who played extras on *Apocalypse Now*. The video installation is an Open Call commission with the Shed in New York and will be showing from October 2023 through January 2024. She works as executive director at Kundiman, a national nonprofit organization dedicated to nurturing writers and readers of Asian American literature.

Lauren Markham is a writer based in California, whose work on social and environmental issues has appeared in outlets such as *Guernica*, *Harper's Magazine*, *The New York Review of Books*, *The New York Times Magazine*, and *VQR*, where she is a contributing editor. She is also the author of an award-winning book, *The Far Away Brothers: Two Young Migrants and the Making of an American Life*, and the forthcoming *A Map of Future Ruins: On Borders and Belonging*, out in spring 2024.

Mallika Rao is a writer living in Brooklyn, New York.

Camille Rankine is the author of *Incorrect Merciful Impulses*, published in 2016 by Copper Canyon Press, and the chapbook *Slow Dance with Trip Wire*, selected by Cornelius Eady for the Poetry Society of America's 2010 New York Chapbook Fellowship. She was the winner of the Discovery Poetry Contest, and is a recipient of fellowships from the National Endowment for the Arts, the Bread Loaf Writers' Conference, and MacDowell. She serves as cochair of the Brooklyn Book Festival Literary Council, and is an assistant professor at Carnegie Mellon University.

Clara Sankey is a writer, editor, and audio producer living in Melbourne, Australia.

Sam Sax is the author of *PIG* (Scribner, 2023), *Yr Living / Yr Dead* (McSweeney's, 2024), *Madness* (Penguin Poets, 2017), and *Bury It* (Wesleyan University Press, 2018). Sam's received fellowships from the National Endowment for the Arts, the Academy of American Poets, and Yaddo, and is currently an ITALIC Lecturer at Stanford University.

Ruby Sutton is a writer from Minnesota. Her work appears in *Astra*, *Hobart Pulp*, *The Mars Review of Books*, and *T Magazine*.

Amanda Uhle is the publisher and executive director of McSweeney's.

Deb Olin Unferth is the author of six books, including the novel *Barn 8*. She has received a Guggenheim Fellowship and four Pushcart Prizes and was a finalist for the National Book Critics Circle Award. A professor at the University of Texas at Austin, she also directs the Pen City Writers, a small creative-writing program at a South Texas penitentiary.

Anne K. Yoder is the author of the novel *The Enhancers*. Her writing has appeared in *Fence*, *BOMB*, and *NY Tyrant*, and has been recognized in *The Best American Nonrequired Reading*. She is the author of two poetry chapbooks and is a member of the Chicago-based publishing and arts collective Meekling Press.

UP NEXT: THE MUSIC ISSUE

Featuring a companion soundtrack, curated by the issue's contributors, and broadcast on BFF.fm

In Search of Wholeness with BTS . . . . Mimi Lok
How Jung's idea of "the shadow self" inspired the world's most famous K-pop superstars.

A Brief and Annoying History of the Kazoo . . . . Paul Collins
First patented in 1883, the kazoo has been irritating Americans for nearly two centuries now. And yet, for reasons no one quite understands, and against great odds, it endures.

The Art of the Ruse . . . . Fernando Flores
In 2006, a history of funerary musicians was put out by a major publisher, alongside an album of "historic compositions." Shortly after their release, the entire thing was exposed as a hoax—but who was behind it, and why?

SOLUTIONS TO THIS ISSUE'S GAMES AND PUZZLES

CROSSWORD
(Page 108)

S	K	A	T	E		S	L	A	V		C	O	L	A
O	N	T	A	P		N	O	T	E	P	A	P	E	R
T	U	T	T	I		O	P	E	R	A	N	E	W	S
T	R	E	A	S	U	R	E	I	S	L	A	N	D	
O	L	D	R	O	M	E		N	E	E	D			
			D	A	F	T		L	O	A	D	E	D	
H	O	U	S	E		E	R	I	E		D	I	V	A
I	S	T	H	I	S	S	E	A	T	T	A	K	E	N
G	L	E	E		I	T	E	M		H	Y	E	N	A
H	O	P	E	S	O		S	L	O	E				
			T	H	U	S		E	D	A	M	A	M	E
H	A	P	A	X	L	E	G	O	M	E	N	O	N	
F	I	N	A	L	S	A	L	E		I	C	A	N	T
P	H	O	N	E	I	T	I	N		S	H	I	E	R
S	O	N	S		E	Y	E	D		H	A	S	T	Y

COPYEDITING THE CLASSICS
(Page 109)

It occurred to me that she expected a response. The sweet, (1) vanilla flavor was still on my tongue and her reading was a wonder in my ears. I had to speak.

I said, "Yes ma'am." (2) It was the least I could do, but it was the most also.

"There's one more thing. Take this book of poems and memorize one for me. Next time you pay me a visit, I want you to recite."

I have tried often to search behind the sophistication of years for the enchantment I so easily found in those gifts. The essence escapes but its aura remains. To be allowed, no, invited, into the private lives of strangers, and to share their joys and fears (3) was a chance to exchange the southern (4) bitter wormwood for a cup of mead with *Beowulf* (5) or a hot cup of tea and milk with Oliver Twist. When I said aloud, "It is a far, far better thing that I do, than I have ever done…" Tears (6) of love filled my eyes at my selflessness.

On that first day, I ran down the hill and into the road (few cars ever came along it) and had the good sense to stop running before I reached the Store (7).

I was liked, and what a difference it made. I was respected not as Mrs. Henderson's grandchild or Bailey's sister but for just being Marguerite Johnson.

Childhood's logic never asks to be proved (all conclusions are absolute). I didn't question why Mrs. Flowers had singled me out for attention, nor did it occur to me that Momma may (8) have asked her to give me a little talking to. All I cared about was that she had made tea cookies for *me* and read to *me* from her favorite book. It was enough to prove that she liked me.

Momma and Bailey were waiting inside the Store. He said, "My, what did she give you?" He had seen the books, but I held the paper sack with his cookies in my arms shielded by the poems.

Momma sighed (9), "Sister, I know you acted like a little lady. That do my heart good to see settled people take to you all. I'm trying my best, the Lord knows, but these days—(10)" Her voice trailed off. "Go on in and change your dress."

1. Delete comma between the non-coordinate adjectives *sweet* and *vanilla*: their order can't be switched without changing the meaning, and an *and* can't be inserted between them 2. "Yes, ma'am." A comma is needed before a name or title used in direct address. 3. Insert a comma here to bracket the aside "and to share in their joys and fears." 4. Southern: capitalize as an adjective in reference to the culture of the South, rather than as a direction 5. Beowulf (roman): this is a reference to the character, not to the book title. 6. tears: lowercase, as this is the second part of the clause beginning "When I said aloud…" 7. *Store* is capped in the original here and below; this is not a typo. 8. might: simple past tense of *may* 9. said: one can't sigh dialogue; *sigh* is considered an action beat, and can't be used as a dialogue tag. 10. Change the em dash to an ellipsis to indicate trailing speech; the em dash signals an interruption.

JACKET CAPTCHA
(Page 110)

1. *No One is Talking About This* by Patricia Lockwood
2. *Cool For You* by Eileen Myles
3. *100 Boyfriends* by Brontez Purnell
4. *The Wallcreeper* by Nell Zink
5. *Blind Willow, Sleeping Woman* by Haruki Murakami
6. *Enormous Changes at the Last Minute* by Grace Paley
7. *A Fan's Notes* by Frederick Exley
8. *An Untamed State* by Roxane Gay
9. *What We Talk About When We Talk About Love* by Raymond Carver

COMPLETE ME
(Page 111)

1) Maine
2) ministers
3) washed away in a flood
4) German Shepherd
5) Shadrach
6) Aslan
7) Noa
8) Sonoran desert tortoises
9) Navy
10) shark attacks
11) typewriters
12) sunglasses
13) guidebook to the Florida Keys
14) Jaguar XK-150